PSYCHOTHERAPY WITH THE UNATTACHED

PSYCHOTHERAPY WITH THE UNATTACHED

Resolving Problems of Single People

by

Herbert S. Strean, D.S.W.

JASON ARONSON INC.
Northvale, New Jersey
London

This book was set in 11 point Palacio by TechType of Upper Saddle River, New Jersey.

Library of Congress Cataloging-in-Publication Data

Strean, Herbert S.
   Psychotherapy with the unattached : resolving problems of single people / by Herbert S. Strean.
      p.   cm.
   Includes bibliographical references and index.
   ISBN 1-56821-539-8 (softcover : alk. paper)
   1. Single people–Mental health. 2. Psychotherapy. I. Title.
   [DNLM: 1. Interpersonal Relations. 2. Psychosexual Dysfunctions–diagnosis. 3. Psychosexual Dysfunctions – therapy.
   4. Psychotherapy. 5. Single Person–psychology.   WM 611 S914p 1995]
   RC451.4.S55S77   1995
   616.89'14'08652 – dc20
   DNLM/DLC
   for Library of Congress   95-4321

Manufactured in the United States of America. Jason Aronson Inc. offers books and cassettes. For information and catalog write to Jason Aronson Inc., 230 Livingston Street, Northvale, New Jersey 07647.

To Marcia
You fill my heart with gladness
It takes away the sadness

With love

Contents

Introduction

In recent decades the institution of marriage has been demeaned and devalued by both professionals and lay persons. Along with this cynicism society now permits more alternatives to conventional marriage than at any previous point in history. A superficial glance at our own society reveals open marriages, unmarried couples living together, bisexual marriages, homosexual marriages, and celibate marriages, to name a few. Mental health professionals agree that one of the many challenges of the 1990s is the need to empathize with and treat sensitively the rich diversity of individuals who have drastically different life-styles.

Despite the fact that modern marriage has many discon

tents, mental health professionals, regardless of the setting in which they practice, the theories they espouse, or the therapeutic modalities they prefer, all concur on one essential fact: their modal patient is the unattached single man or woman. Sometimes unattached men or women appear at the therapist's office experiencing desperation, dejection, and depression. Occasionally they are abusing drugs or alcohol. Not infrequently they boast that the men or women they befriend are passionately in love with them but they themselves can never get "turned on." Some of them are divorced, many have never been married, not a few flee from one relationship to another. Yet, they share one thing—a deep yearning for a partner, and a conviction that the single life is unfulfilling.

Although the popular literature is replete with books, articles, and columns on advice to the lovelorn, the situation is quite different in the professional psychotherapeutic literature. Professional books and articles on marital conflict and marital counseling abound, but with the exception of some literature on therapeutic work with unattached AIDS victims, there is very little material on the dynamics, psychosexual conflicts, and treatment of the single unattached man or woman.

Given that the modal patient of the 1990s is single and unattached, and given also that there is limited literature on his or her dynamics and available treatment, how is this apparent paradox to be resolved? In posing this question to many colleagues of many different persuasions, theoretical perspectives, years of training, and experience, I have invariably received the same response:

"Most clinicians feel very protective of their 'neutral position.' To aver that the unattached person is suffering from internal and interpersonal conflicts and needs treatment is to appear too authoritarian, rigid, dogmatic, insensitive, and therefore, anti-therapeutic." It would appear that many clinicians are failing to differentiate between imposing solutions on their patients (which is almost always contraindicated in sound therapy) and recognizing with them in an empathetic manner that their lonely state is painful and its dynamics and history need to be better understood.

This book takes the unequivocal position that to love and be loved by a mate is a healthier, more fulfilling, more pleasureful modus vivendi than to live alone. There is now sufficient empirical evidence to demonstrate that no man or woman can be an independent island and concomitantly feel happy. Indices of interpersonal conflict and psychological stress are consistently higher among the unmarried. For example, the unmarried die younger than the married, and among the unmarried, heart disease is almost double the rate it is for the married (Lynch 1977). Seagraves (1982) has documented that the highest admission rates to mental hospitals are among the single, divorced, and separated. Like many other researchers, he has pointed out that the unattached are overrepresented in all therapeutic facilities—mental health clinics, mental institutions, and social agencies.

To be sure, a sustained, intimate relationship with a member of the opposite sex is not viewed by all mental health professionals as an index of mental health, and many believe that it is possible to live a fulfilling life outside of a permanent relationship.

Nonetheless, the unattached state has been insufficiently explored in the therapeutic literature. Therefore my purposes in writing this book are several. First, I would like to review and explain the many different dynamic constellations that comprise the single, unattached population. Second, I want to describe the unique psychosexual development of these individuals and demonstrate how their single state is frequently a consequence of unresolved psychosexual tasks. Third, I would like to suggest specific therapeutic principles that my colleagues and I have found useful in helping unattached patients resolve their conflicts and move into a mutually loving relationship with a partner.

Chapter 1 briefly reviews the institution of marriage from the time of Adam and Eve to the present. I will try to demonstrate that there has never been a golden age of marriage. Lovers like Romeo and Juliet, and Tristan and Isolde have been overromanticized and overidealized. Marital partners have always had difficulty tempering their hatred toward each other and learning to love each other. That chapter also attempts to demonstrate how our culture, which emphasizes hedonism and narcissism, does not offer the fertile soil to help marriages grow in harmony. I will suggest that the problem of the unattached, whose numbers keep growing, is in part a cultural phenomenon.

As already stated, I believe that the phenomenon of the unattached man or woman evolves mainly from his or her unresolved psychosexual conflicts. Therefore, in Chapter 2 I will attempt to demonstrate that this patient may suffer from problems at some or all levels of psychosexual development. For example, some may lack what Erikson (1950) has referred to as "the capacity to trust." Others cannot accept "no" for an answer and are involved in constant power struggles with their potential mates. Still others have serious sexual conflicts and are unable to enjoy a stable sexual identity. Many have not resolved problems with their own parents, with whom they are still struggling even though in many instances their parents are no longer living.

In Chapter 2 I will also elaborate on the falling-in-love process and attempt to show that part of sustaining a loving relationship is being able to accept the inevitable disillusionments that accompany it. Here, I demonstrate that many types of immature love emanate from unresolved psychosexual conflicts such as clinging love, sadistic love, rescuing love, unrequited love, and celibate love.

One of the main reasons for my enthusiasm in writing this book is to share with the reader the therapeutic principles I have found to be most valuable in helping the sad and unattached become happily attached. Chapter 3 covers some of the unique features in their assessment and treatment. For example, in their first interviews, many patients often behave with the therapist in the same manner as they do on a first date. Thus, the clinician has to be alert for signs of the patient feeling rejected and/or inducing feelings of rejection in the therapist.

Another important therapeutic principle in working with the unattached patient is that in gathering psychosocial data, it is important to get a very full picture of the prospective patient's early interpersonal relationships. The clinician eventually can show the patient how he or she tends to recapitulate old self-destructive relationships in the present.

If we can get a full, early psychosocial picture and make an accurate diagnostic assessment of his or her conflicts, ego strengths and limitations, superego pressures, impact of his or her history, social context, and other variables, we can then make a carefully individualized diagnostic assessment and treatment plan.

One of the important points discussed in Chapter 3 is that chronic complaints about prospective partners are really unconscious wishes. The unattached man, for example, who constantly complains that his female partners do not turn him on, does not want to be turned on. Sexual feelings, warmth, and intimacy frighten him. Similarly, the unattached woman who constantly refers to her partners as "wimps" wants her men to be weak and impotent. Somebody more attractive and more potent would frighten her.

Another crucial therapeutic principle discussed in Chapter 3, and stressed throughout the text, is that if the therapist does not take sides in the patient's interpersonal problems, does not praise or criticize the patient's partners or behavior, the patient's interpersonal struggles will emerge in the transference relationship. For example, the patient who idealizes the therapist and feels like a helpless child with him or her, will be doing the same with prospective mates. As the patient sees himself or herself repeating behaviors with the therapist that he or she has shown with prospective partners, the patient begins to gain some conviction about his or her own role contributing to interpersonal problems.

In addition to demonstrating how to resolve transference, resistance, countertransference, and counterresistance issues in work with the unattached, Chapter 3 also demonstrates the appropriateness of different therapeutic modalities: short-term work, crisis intervention, couples counseling, and long-term treatment. Although the focus of this book is largely on one-to-one long-term treatment, other therapeutic approaches that can help the unattached will be considered.

Chapters 4 through 7 present four intensive case discussions of unattached men and women who came for therapy, resolved their problems, and moved into happy marriages. These case discussions utilize many of the theoretical constructs that were discussed in Chapters 1 through 3.

Chapter 8 is composed of case illustrations of single individuals who came for couples counseling. Here, I demonstrate how couple's counseling is similar to and different from one-to-one treatment. Finally, in Chapter 9, I review what the individuals described in this book have in common, for example, strong resentments toward the opposite sex, unresolved dependency needs, and sexual inhibitions. I also summarize the unique therapeutic principles that were particularly helpful to these individuals.

I would like to thank the many individuals whose help has been most valuable in writing this book, for without such help this project would never have reached the light of day. First and foremost, I would like to thank my wife Marcia, who edited and typed this book. For over forty years, her love and support have made seemingly difficult projects like writing books lots of fun!

Dr. Jason Aronson and members of his staff, Dr. Michael Moskowitz, Norma Pomerantz, and Judy Cohen, as always, have provided sound editorial assistance and many laughs.

Finally, I would like to thank the many single, unattached patients who sought my help and provided me with many valuable insights. The longer I am in this field, the more I believe that our patients are our best consultants and supervisors.

1

Wither Marriage or Whither Marriage?

When unattached men and women visit a therapist's office for their first encounter, after telling the clinician about their depressed feelings, somatic symptoms, insomnia, lack of satisfaction in interpersonal relations, and a pervasive feeling of emptiness, they eventually get to talk about their constant feeling of loneliness and longing for a partner. As the clinician helps them to describe the kind of partner they are looking for and how the latter will enhance their lives, they begin to feel a sense of hope. An empathetic therapist who accepts them warmly and does not threaten them with demands or advice, helps unattached men and women consider the possibility that an intimate relationship may not be so onerous.

Just as such individuals often feel optimistic and enthusiastic when they begin a relationship with a prospective partner only to find fault with the new acquaintance after a few meetings, the same phenomenon inevitably occurs in therapy. Hope sooner or later turns to dread, enthusiasm is replaced by cynicism, those dimensions of marriage once seen as pleasureful begin to appear painful, and the therapist initially experienced as a catalyst and facilitator is now viewed as an insensitive obstacle.

Quite frequently the unattached person has tried many different forms of help before turning to psychotherapy. This patient has probably been answering "personals" in magazines and possibly has placed a few advertisements in local newspapers or other media. Most likely he or she has attended "single weekends" at hotels, and has gone to churches or synagogues for dances that cater to "single men and women from 25–45 who are looking for a partner." When such encounters have yielded limited success, and when encounter groups, sensitivity training, and bio-feedback have not helped, psychotherapy may be considered. And when psychotherapy tends to appear similar to previous unfulfilling experiences, the patient becomes very bitter and not only castigates the therapist, but becomes very critical of the institution of marriage, elaborating its pitfalls and limitations.

"Divorces keep going up in number," a 35-year-old male patient correctly asserts in his third month of weekly therapy. "I don't think I want to be part of that group of ex-husbands who spend half their income on alimony," he angrily concludes. A 29-year-old attractive woman in her sixth month of twice-weekly treatment avers, "In this day and age it's so difficult to determine how a woman can get along well with a man. Gender roles are in transition and who is to say what is appropriate or inappropriate?" A 38-year-old divorced woman in her seventh month of three-times-a-week psychoanalysis explodes in anger and fearfully declares, "My biological clock is wearing down. I want a child but many men are frightened of becoming fathers. What the hell is a father supposed to do in this age of supposed equality? Shouldn't he stay home and watch the kids—at least some of the time?"

Usually, disenchanted and disillusioned patients, after offering many valid criticisms of the institution of marriage, begin to reflect on the marital interaction of their parents and grandparents. More often than not these patients conclude, "Though they didn't get divorced, they were not that happy. There was a subtle tension in the home most of the time that was never talked about."

A typical example of an unattached patient is the following vignette of Jim, whose treatment is described briefly.

Jim O'Connor, an accountant in New York City, came to see me when he was 35 years old. Approximately six feet tall and heavy set, Jim walked into my office with a slow stride and spoke initially in a quiet manner. "Although I do pretty well in my work, I don't get along too well with people on the outside. Most women reject me and men just tolerate me," Jim confided in his first interview. His deep depression and self-hatred were noticeable within the first five minutes of the session.

Although Jim was a graduate of a prestigious university and had a master's degree in business administration, he derived little pleasure from his accomplishments. No sooner had he informed me about his education than he went on to tell me that his father was a bus driver and his mother was a waitress. He commented, "I guess I'm quite ashamed of my background. My father can barely read. My mother reads true romance magazines and both of my sisters are emotional cripples."

Before seeking me out, Jim had consulted several other therapists. He described these therapists, all men, as "responsible professionals who just couldn't help me." When I asked Jim for more details of his previous therapeutic experiences, it became clear, as it usually does with patients who have had several therapists, that Jim had a latent contempt for his previous helpers and secretly wished to defeat them.

As I listened to Jim's previous experiences, I began to hypothesize that just as he had related to them in a sadomasochistic, self-destructive manner and achieved limited results, so had his relationships with women (and men, too) been destructive. He reminded me of a description that the psychoanalyst Kohut (1971, 1977) made frequently when describing self-destructive patients as "an empty self." This is an individual who is "depressed and without vigor." I wondered also during my first interview with Jim how long it would take before he would tire of me. Considering his fragile interpersonal relationships, I was not confident I had much of a chance to sustain a relationship with him. "Nobody else had done too well. Why should I?" I asked myself.

Jim surprised me. He liked my non-judgmental, quiet listening and after a month of therapy said, "The other guys talked too much, wanted to convince me of things, but you just seem like 'old reliable,' who is interested in hearing what I have to say and I think you care." Jim seemed to experience the beginning phase of the therapy as if he were in "a holding environment" (Winnicott 1971), a place where the child in him was being nurtured.

For several months in his twice-weekly therapy, Jim spoke a great deal about his hurt from and anger toward his parents and siblings. "They never offered much stimulation or support," he said tearfully. By his third month in treatment he had his first major insight when he commented, "I seem to resent the world as if all it consisted of was my family members."

Because I continued to listen to Jim without censuring him or trying to convince him of anything, he felt accepted by me and began to feel warmly toward me. As a result his depression seemed to diminish.

Our "therapeutic honeymoon" (Fine 1982) lasted five months. During that time he dated women who did not walk out on him. He made more money at work and bought expensive, attractive clothes. He had no trouble, as he sometimes had before, in performing sexually.

As is true with all honeymoons, Jim's eventually ended. One day during the sixth month of treatment, he missed an appointment, giving no excuse for his absence. When I said, "In the future, I'll have to charge you for missed appointments," Jim's reaction was very powerful. With his face as red as a beet and a voice ringing with anger, this man who just a month before told me, "You are the greatest guy who ever lived," now said, "You cheap bastard. You are a whore. You operate like a whore. You charge money and think you are loving people. I don't think I can be associated with someone as greedy and selfish as you." From an idealizing transference (Kohut 1971), Jim had dramatically changed his position and virtually wanted to kill me.

Although I previously prided myself on my ability to cope with patients' put-downs with equanimity, I found Jim's remarks very difficult to bear. I experienced him as a big bully from my childhood.

During Jim's tirades toward me, he also berated every other therapist in America. He also told me that I was as untrustworthy "as the stupid dames" he dated. He not only condemned women, but went on to condemn the institution of marriage and ridiculed anybody who advocated "an intimate relationship."

As I tried to monitor my own rage and attempted to empathize with Jim's basic mistrust I could more and more appreciate his deep sense of vulnerability. When I put myself emotionally into Jim's "frigid" childhood home and felt his despair, he somehow began to sense that maybe I was not his enemy.

In Jim's thirteenth month of therapy he had a dream in which we were drinking some wine together. In the fourteenth month of treatment, although frightened and embarrassed, he shared some homosexual fantasies that he had toward me. When he saw I did not deride him for those fantasies but wanted to understand them better, Jim was able to spend the next few months talking about his deep yearning for love, which had always terrified him. The more he could talk about his deep wish to be loved and cared for, the less infantile narcissism he showed in his daily behavior. His sadomasochism began to wane and after two years of therapy, his relaxed attitude toward me began to carry over to other relationships in his life. He fell in love with a woman three years his junior who was a college teacher. Within six months they married and, soon after, Jim successfully terminated his treatment.

Although each unattached patient who visits a therapist's office is a special person with a unique history and dynamics, and therefore requires an individualized treatment plan, he/she is also a product of his/her culture and its history where the institution of marriage is in deep trouble and never has been out of trouble!

In this chapter, I would like briefly to review the history of marriage and then consider how the marital institution appears to be shaping up in the 1990s. Perhaps we can then gain a better perspective on some of the plight of the unattached.

Marriage: An Historical Prespective

Ever since the beginning of recorded time, marriage has been considered an essential institution in every known society. In the Bible we learn that Eve had her Adam, Abraham had his Sarah, and most of the kings had their queens.

Despite the ubiquity of marriage, and although there have been many different forms and practices characterizing marriage over the centuries, it is virtually impossible to point to any historical era or culture where the majority of husbands and wives consistently loved each other. As Demos (1976), in his paper "Myths and Realities in the History of American Family Life," has pointed out, there never was a Golden Age of Marriage gleaming at us from the historical past.

In *The Natural History of Love*, Morton Hunt (1959) shows that by the seventh century church dogma had established that erotic feelings between husband and wife were incompatible with the spiritual side of marriage. Robert Barker (1984) in his research on early marriage discovered written remnants from early civilizations such as Babylonia, Egypt, and Judea reveal that marriage was little more than an institution by which to subjugate women. A woman was property, possessed first by her father, then by her husband, and finally by her son.

In ancient Rome, where equality between the sexes was valued, the results were not too favorable either. Divorce became popular and family life decayed. And, when the ancient Greeks experimented with "open marriage"—one of the first societies to do so—family life was disrupted. Adultery, homosexuality, and prostitution became popular; warm, marital interaction was little observed (Barker 1984, Hunt 1959).

Occasionally, some historians mistakenly refer to the era of romantic love as an exceptional period when men and women genuinely loved each other and fused tender and erotic impulses. However, a more careful examination of this epoch yields the same picture as before. Although lovers like Romeo and Juliet, Tristan and Isolde, Antony and Cleopatra, and Cyrano and Roxanne are associated with romantic love, it should be remembered that most of these lovers, unlike most husbands and wives, lived apart, probably did not participate in sex, and had limited emotional interaction—at times almost none. When individuals live apart, they tend to fantasize more and are able to shun the limitations that reality imposes on them.

The world in which romantic love was born was a world where violence was everywhere and fully rationalized (Bloch 1961). War, murder, and the abuse of power were everpresent threats that affected everyone's life (Hay 1975). As Reuben Fine (1985) in *The Meaning of Love in Human Experience* has suggested, romantic love was an attempt to subdue some of the violence that was characteristic of that period. Part of the code of the "gentleman" involved the refusal to inflict harm on a woman. The man was supposed to adopt a protective attitude toward the woman in which his own safety was secondary to her welfare. The woman was elevated to the place of a "lady," but behind this chivalry and by putting his lady on a pedestal and worshipping her from afar, the man denied and repressed his anger and in many ways became a young boy with a mother figure.

American society has been a hate culture since its inception (Fine 1985). And in societies that preceded ours, competition between human beings was more valued than cooperation, egocentrism was more dominant than altruism, and violence was more pervasive than peaceful interaction. Although the human race has made much progress in many areas of endeavor such as science, technology, and engineering, there has been little positive movement in learning how to foster and sustain loving, peaceful interaction between human beings. Religion has had little effect on the hatreds that seethe in men's and women's minds, and the many social and political movements such as socialism, communism, and capitalism have had limited positive effect.

As social scientists, particularly historians, have begun to examine critically the relationships between husbands and wives over the centuries (DeMause 1981, Fine 1985, Shorter 1975, Stone 1979), evidence has emerged that strongly suggests that there has been little love between spouses. As Shorter (1975) states: "On the farm, man and wife got along in quiet hostility and withdrawal" (p. 33). In 1748, the weekly paper of the small Prussian town of Halle attempted a statistical estimate: scarcely ten marriages in 1000 were happy ones, while in all the others "the spouses cursed and bemoaned their choices" (Shorter 1975, p. 51). We also learn from that source that wives usually did not share meals with their husbands, often standing behind them and acting as servants. Shorter also points out that contempt for women was so strong that the loss of a stable animal caused more grief for the peasant than the loss of his wife.

Although by the nineteenth century, there were many more happy marriages than reported in previous centuries, there were many problems as well. As Fine (1985) has stated:

> . . . the image of pure unsullied bliss came under severe attack until it was finally shattered by Sigmund Freud. Nineteenth century marriage repressed sex, blocked spontaneity, enforced a cruel regimen on children, and was often honoured more in the breach than in the observance. Man was still master of the house, woman his devoted slave. In many countries women still had almost no legal rights; they could not work, so that they had the choice only of being housewives or prostitutes (and prostitution flourished on an enormous scale). [pp. 99–100]

As late as the early twentieth century, Havelock Ellis (1907) quoted Dr. William Hammond, the Surgeon General of the United States, as saying that it was doubtful most women enjoyed marriage and that maybe one-tenth of them enjoyed sex with their husbands.

Although the modern family has emerged as an ideal, the realities are entirely different and the hate culture that has dominated western civilization for 2500 years has not shown appreciable change.

Marriage in the 1990s

In *Neurotic Interaction in Marriage* (Eisenstein 1956), anthropologist Ashley Montagu stated, "Neurotic interaction takes place essentially between individuals, but the nature of the individuals and of the marriage itself cannot be thoroughly understood without some understanding of their cultural and societal context" (pp. 3–4).

What can we say about the culture of the 1990s that influences marital interaction? Our culture is described by experts in very pejorative terms. The historian Lasch (1978) has referred to our "culture of narcissism" in which men, women, and children are dominated by the pleasure principle and find it difficult to empathize with the struggles and wishes of family and friends. Many social scientists have agreed (De Burger 1978, Fine 1981, Grunebaum and Christ 1976, Hendin 1975) that ours is a hedonistic society where sexual aggrandizement is extolled and self-interest, that is, narcissism, is championed. To offer some proof of this, in the popular media we are advised to be our own best friend, promote our self-interest, and gratify our own impulses. Self-help books are best sellers and television commercials offer magical solutions to gratify the viewers' grandiose wishes.

The emphasis on narcissism and hedonism in our culture influences marital interaction. When individuals want instant gratification, they become angry and exasperated when their marital partners do not gratify their omnipotent and narcissistic yearnings. Testimony to the low level of frustration tolerance and fury of spouses is the popularity of newspaper columns full of vitriolic complaints from husbands and wives who feel deprived and unfulfilled (Strean 1985).

Herbert Hendin (1975), a psychoanalyst who has

studied the impact of cultural forces on individual behavior, has referred to our current era as "The Age of Sensation." According to Hendin, men, women, and children in our society are so exclusively concerned with their own primitive desires that they find it too difficult to maturely love another human being. He has contended that the high rate of divorce, separation, and feuding among the married reflects the cultural trend toward replacing commitment, involvement, and tenderness with self-aggrandizement, exploitation, and titillation—characteristics of Fine's (1981, 1985) "hate culture."

Shachter and Seinfeld (1994) have referred to our society as "a culture of violence."

> The American culture of violence is reflected in the history, attitudes, belief systems, and coping styles of the population in dealing with conflicts, frustration, and the quest for wealth and power. Historically, violent traditions have made a clear imprint. Recall the genocidal wars against Native Americans by the early settlers; the lawlessness of the American frontier; the violence of slavery; the fratricidal Civil War; the massacres of early union organizers; the long history of violence against racial, ethnic, and political minorities; the violence against women; the romanticizing of the gangsters of the Roaring Twenties; and the imperialistic wars against Third World countries.
>
> More recently we have seen growing personal violence among U.S. citizens. Manifestations of such escalation are widespread. Homicide rates among black men ages 15 to 24 rose two-thirds in the five years through 1988. . . . Homicide is the leading

cause of death among black males ages 15–24. . . .
The possession of hand guns is increasing . . . and, in
addition, manifestations of violence on television and
film have grown. Violence sells. . . . [p. 347]

Regardless of who is the aggressor, research has shown
that more people are likely to be killed, physically as-
saulted, beaten up, slapped, or spanked in their own
homes more than anywhere else (Fine 1988). Gelles (1972)
has proposed that violence in the family is more common
than love.

Although the issue of the battered wife has assumed
prominence, the battered husband is now being given
consideration as well. In *Wife Beating: The Silent Crisis*,
Langley and Levy (1977) reported that one-fifth of the
married women in America beat their husbands, though
few of the men admitted it.

For an immature culture like ours, which considers
narcissism a virtue, it is inevitable that marriage and
family life are deteriorating. As President Clinton has
warned us, we cannot renew our country when, within a
decade, more than half of our children will be born into
families where there is no marriage.

Blurring of Gender Roles

The 1990s reflect a continuing turmoil about which
norms regarding marriage ought to be upheld. Although
there is a new trend to conceptualize sexual roles in
essentially biological terms, such as in the best-seller
Anatomy of Love by Helen Fisher (1993), in which the author
provides many biological answers to questions concerning

gender roles, most clinicians look to the cultural context to provide answers.

As early as 1935, the anthropologist Margaret Mead concluded that the definitions of male and female varied from culture to culture. In her well-known book *Sex and Temperament in Three Primitive Societies*, Mead (1935) showed that each culture evolved a different conception of what is "naturally" feminine and what is "naturally" masculine. Her major conclusion was that the determinants of masculinity and femininity in any culture are more cultural than biological. Stated Mead: "The material suggests that many, if not all, of the personality traits which we have called masculine or feminine are as tightly linked to sex as are the clothing, the manners and the form of headdress that a society at a given period assigns to either sex" (p. 206).

As we look at our current culture, there is more blurring of gender roles than at any previous time in our history. As opposed to earlier times, there is neither a clear-cut division of labor nor clear-cut prescriptions for the roles of husband and wife. Over 50 percent of married women are now working. Many of them are in positions that previous generations of men thought were theirs exclusively. In the 1990s we not only have women wearing judges' robes or corporate pinstripes, but we also have women attired in Dayglo prison jumpsuits. According to the Justice Department, the number of women in state and federal prisons increased 256 percent from 1980 to 1990. This is compared with a 140 percent growth in the male prison population.

When husbands and wives are unsure of their appropriate roles, competition and power struggles become more prominent in their day-to-day interactions with each other; mutual gratification diminishes, and loneliness in both becomes intensified.

The inability of men and women to reconcile the inconsistencies in their role sets has caused many individuals and groups to claim that marriage is too complicated and constricting for personality development, is emotionally crippling to one or both partners, and provides a setting for mutual exploitation (DeBurger 1978). Some groups in the women's movement argue that a woman who commits herself to one man is collaborating in her own oppression (Durbin 1977) and that traditional marriage is a form of serfdom or slavery (Smith and Smith 1974). Many writers emphasize that masturbation and lesbianism are acceptable routes to sexual gratification for women and are superior to heterosexual intercourse (Hite 1983). The comedian Groucho Marx was quoted as saying, "Marriage is a great institution, but only if you want to live in an institution." The popular writer Jane Howard (1978), in her book *Families*, constantly referred to marriage as a chancy, grim experiment rather than how it is idealized as "an ancient institution."

One of the negative consequences of the blurring of gender roles has been the intensification of sexual problems. Many husbands and wives are reporting "a lack of sexual desire" (Kaplan 1983), and sex therapists of all persuasions are doing a booming business (Strean 1985). It may be hypothesized, however, that in the 1990s, married individuals feel an increased freedom and legitimate right to face their sexual problems than heretofore, and that is why lack of sexual fulfillment has become such a salient issue. In 1896, Sigmund Freud opined that it would take humanity 100 years to come to terms with the claims of sexuality. He also pointed out at that time how seldom normal potency was to be found in a husband and how often frigidity was found in a wife.

What are we to conclude about marriage in the 1990s? It can be safely said that current married men and women do not appear to be healthier and happier than their forebears. Among the married, regardless of the form the marriage takes (open marriage, celibate marriage, commuter marriage), suicide rates are high, alcoholism is pervasive, violence and abuse has intensified, and anxiety is rampant (Fine 1992, Serban 1981). The "open marriage" of the 1990s is no more harmonious than it was when the Greeks invented it centuries ago, and the sexual revolution of the 1960s and 1970s has not brought any more satisfaction than it did to the ancient Romans. Married life in the 1990s is not fulfilling for many.

If life for the married in the 1990s is very difficult, it is even more difficult for the unattached. As we suggested in the introduction to this book, among the unmarried (the divorced, widowed, and the single) all indices of interpersonal conflict; suicide, alcoholism, violence, and abuse are higher among the unattached than among the attached. The highest admission rates to mental hospitals are among single, divorced, and separated people (Fine 1988, Seagraves 1982).

If being married is an unhappy and unfulfilling state of

being for many husbands and wives in the 1990s, unmarried life can be described as acutely lonely and very stressful for the unattached. Although their numbers are increasing and their pleasures decreasing (Fine 1988, 1992), thousands of unattached men and women are seeking psychotherapy so that they can learn to love and be loved on a sustained basis. Chapter 2 considers those forces and issues that prevent the unattached from becoming attached.

2

The Psychosexual Development of the Unattached Person

In his paper "On Narcissism," Sigmund Freud (1914) presented one of his most brilliant insights. He pointed out that if a man or woman cannot love, he or she will fall ill. Freud was able to demonstrate that if loving feelings, a fusion of tender and erotic impulses, are not directed toward another human being, the man or woman not able to love inevitably becomes a victim of depression or dysfunctions such as hypochondriasis, grandiose fantasies, free floating anxiety, or a host of similar symptoms.

Many years ago Freud discovered a truth that has never been refuted, that is, to love is healthy and mature, not to love is unhealthy and immature.

Many years after Freud's discovery, Rohner (1975), an

anthropologist, was able to demonstrate that children who grew up in societies where they were loved by their parents became contented adults; where they were not loved, they became depressed, unhappy, and resentful people.

The search for love is universal (Fine 1988), even if it is not often realized. Furthermore, love does not come into existence immediately. Love has to grow and be nurtured. Falling in love, as I will show later in this chapter, is a regressive, immature response. Loving, which takes time and effort, is a mature means of coping with life.

How a man or woman expresses, experiences, and receives love is based on the story of his or her life. Loving and being loved in adulthood is in many ways a revival of the real and fantasied love relationships that one experienced during childhood and adolescence.

To understand and help unattached patients in therapy, we have to become sensitive to their psychosexual development. For example, if a child during the first year of life has been unable to learn to trust his or her mother (Erikson 1950) he or she will probably be suspicious of love partners and resist intimate emotional and sexual contacts with them. In effect, the child in all of us remains alive and always affects our adult behavior.

Constitutional Strengths and Limitations

A crucial variable contributing to an individual's personality functioning and a very important factor in determining his or her attachments or lack of them later in life is the person's native endowment. No matter how benign and sensitive an individual's caretakers have been, such phenomena as temperament, intelligence, drive endowment, physical appearance, and many other facets of the human being are shaped much more by genetic influence and play an important role.

Although the color of eyes and hair or the intensity of the drives cannot be appreciably altered by an environmental input, how the individuals in that child's environment respond to the youngster's native endowment will have a powerful effect on self-image and will very much influence the youngster's interaction with others. For example, clinicians are well aware that some parents prefer girls to boys, or vice versa; some mothers and fathers resent energetic children, others love them. Some parents respond positively to tall children, some feel threatened by them.

In *Personal Psychopathology*, Harry Stack Sullivan (1972), an expert on interpersonal relations, pointed out that how we feel about ourselves is largely an introjection of what we believe others have thought of us. If parents have responded positively to our native endowment, we tend to feel the same way. However, if the response was not affirming, our body and self image are negatively affected and this, in turn, influences the quality of our interactions with others.

Arthur, a 29-year-old man, was in once-a-week psychotherapy in a mental health clinic. He sought treatment because he was constantly being rejected by the women he dated. Arthur had an important insight during his sixth month of therapy. He recalled how his father, mother, and brother frequently demeaned him because he was left-handed. They would frequently tell him that he was "way out in left field," his politics were "too left of center," and he should buy a "left-handed monkey wrench."

Arthur introjected the pejorative labels ascribed to him and found himself almost always feeling inept, particularly around mechanical pursuits. This gradually spread to his total self-image; eventually he called himself an "odd ball," particularly when he was around women. He expected to be rejected, and with his self-demeaning attitude, it became a self-fulfilling prophecy. Women rejected him because he seemed extremely self-effacing and masochistic, and therefore unappealing.

Sometimes parents can be too generous with praise and overevaluate their children's native endowment. Most clinicians have learned that children are sometimes experienced as narcissistic extensions by their parents. Consequently, when parents overestimate the abilities or beauty of their children, they are unconsciously lauding themselves excessively.

Beverly was a 32-year-old woman in analysis four times a week. After a year of treatment, she became aware of her tendency to be supercilious and contemptuous of men, as if no man was "good enough" for her.

When Beverly was asked by her therapist to free associate to her demeaning attitude toward men, she recalled how both her parents throughout her childhood told her that she had perfect physical features—height, weight, face, figure, and so forth. Beverly introjected her parents' view of her and related to the world as if she were a princess. She expected men to worship her and cater to her every whim. Her grandiose, highly narcissistic demeanor alienated men and after at least a dozen unhappy love affairs, Beverly sought analysis.

The Oral Stage (Trust vs Mistrust)

The first phase of maturational development has been called the oral period (Freud 1905) because virtually all of the infant's interests center around the mouth. Paramount during most of the first year of life is the baby's wish to be fed and to be made comfortable through nursing.

Direct investigation of children has clearly demonstrated the crucial importance of love for the well-being of the child (Spitz 1965). Loss or withdrawal of an important person is probably the most devastating experience a child can endure, and its effects are disastrous for a later feeling of well-being. The acronym TLC, tender loving care, has become popular as a result of research on child development. If the child has been the recipient of TLC, he or she will in all probability be able to trust another human being and concomitantly feel an inner certainty within.

Many unattached men and women do not form a relationship with a loving partner because they cannot trust the partner. They relate as if the partner were an ungiving mother. They may even unconsciously seek out untrustworthy mates so they can hate them as if the latter were the ungiving mother of their past.

Christopher, a single man of 42, was in treatment for alcoholism. After about nine months of twice-a-week therapy, he learned that he would rather rely on the bottle, "which is always there," rather than "try to trust a woman who is never there." Christopher's mother was a very depressed woman who was unavailable to him during most of his childhood. Thus, Christopher turned away from people for gratification and relied on alcohol instead. He either provoked women to move away from him or sought unreliable women who could not be trusted.

A prerequisite for healthy maturation is weaning. For youngsters to be able to accept the limitations that relationships impose, they need help in giving up the breast and the bottle. As they learn that they cannot have whatever they want whenever they want it, their infantile narcissism and grandiosity are moderated and their frustration tolerance and impulse control become strengthened.

In order to participate in a mutually loving relationship, both partners have to temper their narcissistic, omnipotent yearnings and control their demands. When a child has not been helped to accomplish these maturational tasks, he or she is not able to form a mature attachment to a partner.

Dolores, age 40, had been divorced twice, both of her marriages lasting less then a year. When she was in her second year of intensive therapy and began to explore her childhood, she gained some awareness of how her past contributed to her difficulties in intimate relationships. She described both of her parents as very attentive people who "always gave me everything I wanted." Feeling quite convinced that the whole world was her oyster, she thought she had a legitimate right to insist that her mates be indulgent parents. When they could not incessantly gratify her, she had temper tantrums. Eventually the men became disgusted and left.

When the infant has been helped to relinquish some primary narcissism, he or she moves into a stage described as the symbiotic phase of development. In, *On Human Symbiosis and the Vicissitudes of Individuation*, Margaret Mahler (1968) points out that despite the fact that the symbiosis between mother and infant is mutually pleasureful, a healthy mother–infant dyad advances toward what Mahler refers to as "separation-individuation." If the child feels loved while behaving autonomously, he or she can begin to internalize this positive experience and feel a healthy self-esteem away from the mother.

When children have not been sufficiently helped to separate and individuate, they continue to seek out symbiotic attachments. As adults they insist on being informed about every detail of their partner's daily life and have a strong wish to inform the partner of every detail of their own daily life. If the partner frustrates the individual's symbiotic yearnings, the latter feels hurt, despondent, and very angry. Eventually either one partner feels overwhelmed by the constant demands made and/or the other insisting on 24-hour-a-day togetherness feels so rejected that the relationship deteriorates.

Forty-five-year-old Ed was in therapy for the third time. Although he was very eager to "settle down" and get married, it "never seems to work out."

His female therapist soon became aware of how Ed always wanted to prolong therapy sessions with her, called her frequently between sessions, and constantly wanted to know details of her life. Believing that this was also his tendency in his relations with women, the therapist thought it would be helpful to explore Ed's clinging behavior in therapy.

When asked about his desire for extra-therapeutic contacts, Ed became indignant, contending his behavior reflected his "warm and engaging disposition" and that his therapist was "an excessively shy person."

Although it was very clear to the therapist that Ed's intense desire for a symbiosis with her mirrored his behavior with his women friends, it took Ed close to two years of three-times-a-week therapy before he could just begin to think of his symbiotic behavior as something problematic. It took him another year before he could gain some conviction that his inability to tolerate just one degree of separation from his women partners was the main reason for his remaining unattached.

The English psychiatrist and psychoanalyst John Bowlby has proposed the concept of "anxious attachment" (1973). He refers to a tendency to behave in a way that reflects anxiety over the availability and/or responsiveness of attachment figures. The individual who suffers from anxious attachment lacks confidence that key figures will be accessible if called upon. Thus, he or she is always prone to separation anxiety.

In a paper, "Anxious Attachment in Adulthood: Therapeutic Implications," Pat Sable (1994) has pointed out how separation anxiety that is an integral component of anxious attachments appears frequently in unattached adults. This is apparent in the following case that came to my attention a few years ago.

> Flora, age 40, came into treatment because she wanted to overcome her fear of an intimate relationship with a man. As her life was explored in her therapy, it became clear that as a child she was very neglected by both parents, physically abused, and subjected to all kinds of threats. It took several years of intensive therapy before Flora could believe that men would not hurt or destroy her.

All love relationships for both sexes tend to recapitulate the early mother–infant reaction to some extent. Though not the sole determinant, the oral phase of development seems to establish a lasting association between affection and the need for others. If children have received consistent warmth from an empathetic mother, they will be more inclined to trust themselves and their partners in a loving relationship (Erikson 1950).

The Anal Stage (Autonomy vs Self-Doubt)

If the first year of life has been consistently gratifying and if the child has been able to master the frustrations of being weaned, he or she is ready during the second year of life to assume new developmental tasks. During the second year of life the child should be able to absorb more frustration, take "no" for an answer more often, and learn to control his or her impulses with less difficulty.

The period from one to three years of age has been referred to as the anal stage of development. Because of the physically maturing ability to control the sphincter, the child shifts attention from the oral zone to the anal zone. The anal zone provides further outlets for libidinal gratification, referred to as anal eroticism, and for the emerging aggressive drive characterized as anal sadism (Moore and Fine 1990).

One of the demands placed on a child during the second year of life in most societies is toilet training. This is not usually an easy task for most children to master. Having lived a life of constant gratification during the first year of life, the baby is not eager to change. Having been a receiver most of the time, it is not easy to suddenly become a giver and altruistically deposit urine and fecal matter neatly in the toilet bowl. Taking on responsibility during the second year of life is difficult when the child has been accustomed to having others take over most of the time.

A great deal of ambivalence is characteristic of the child during the training period. Although children out of love for their parents want to please them, they also feel hatred toward them for imposing rules, regulations, and controls that seem to the child unnecessary, harsh, and arbitrary.

When children are unable to resolve their mixed feelings of love and hatred for their parents, they have a strong ambivalence toward love objects as adults. Many adults experience cooperation as submission and resent "doing their duty" for their mates. Many unattached adults get into constant power struggles with potential partners, worried that if they gratify their partners, they are "giving in." They distort love and cooperation, viewing those traits as humiliating and masochistic.

> Gordon, age 51, had been through three marriages and three divorces over a period of twelve years. Although he found it easy to fall in love with women, sooner or later he felt "exploited," "used," and "demeaned." Having sex eventually became "a job" and he became impotent.
>
> In his therapy, Gordon was eventually able to see that he turned women into the controlling mother of his past and began "to hate their guts."

During the second year of life children begin to develop a superego. The superego consists of the conscience that embodies the voices of parents that say "no," and the ego ideal that is the depository of positive, ethical, and moral imperatives—the "yeses." If children are trained harshly and arbitrarily, they, of course, resent it. Moreover, many children reared in a hostile atmosphere become very intimidated by their parents, turn their hostility inward, and develop punitive superegos. If the punitive superego is not modified, the child, as an adult, feels intimidated by his or her partner and feels that no matter what he or she does, "it's never enough."

> Hazel, age 40, an attractive and bright woman, had a series of unsuccessful love affairs. As she described each relationship to her therapist, a recurrent theme emerged. After the man showed a great deal of love and admiration for her,

Hazel felt "eternally grateful" and felt that she "owed the man everything."

The act of reciprocating, for Hazel, was equivalent to "putting out" for her demanding parents. Consequently, she began to resent all that she felt a relationship required and sooner or later withdrew from her mates.

Erik Erikson (1950) conceptualized the conflict of the second year of life as "autonomy versus shame and doubt." If a child does not feel too hostile toward his parents, he is freer to enjoy his or her autonomy and independence. However, if youngsters feel resentment toward their parents, there is a tendency to want to act out revenge each time they are independent. When on their own they harbor fantasies toward their parents and imagine themselves bellowing at Mom and Dad, "Who needs you!"

When youngsters have to cope with a great deal of resentment, they feel ashamed of themselves, doubt their own autonomous capacities, and worry about when they are going to be reprimanded. As adults they cannot tolerate their autonomy nor their partner's.

Ian was a 42-year-old man in psychoanalytic treatment. He told his therapist that every time he was in a relationship with a woman, she "rejected" him. When his therapist explored with Ian the whys and wherefores of the "rejection," it turned out that whenever his woman friend had to do something away from him, he experienced this as a personal rebuke. One of the main reasons he misinterpreted his women friends' independence and saw it as a rebuke was because this was what he felt he was doing to her, when on his own, that is, rebuking her.

Ian's distortion of autonomy had its roots in his childhood. Raised in a strict, controlling atmosphere, he harbored strong hostile fantasies of escaping from it. However, any time he was away from home, he thought he would return to find his parents dead—a dreaded wish come true.

If a youngster has been severely toilet trained, he or she becomes pissed off and/or wants to shit all over the place. As an adult, this individual will have a tendency to demean and castigate the partner, often treating the latter "like shit." Obviously, this type of modus vivendi does not win friends or positively influence prospective partners. The angry, rebellious child becomes the sad, unattached man or woman.

When mature adults have not resolved the problems of the second year of life, their conflicts frequently appear in their sexual lives. Because they tend to experience their sex partners as the selfish and controlling parents of their past, they do not want to gratify them sexually, nor can they derive much pleasure from them.

If adults have to cope with unmastered sadistic fantasies, in sexual intercourse they may unconsciously want to urinate or defecate on their partners. Consequently, they either inhibit their sexual desires because they are frightened of becoming too cruel, or they become selfish, inconsiderate lovers full of angry demands.

Jessica was a single 35-year-old woman who was in therapy because she received very limited gratification from her sexual relationships. As she reviewed her childhood, what emerged was that she was toilet-trained at 7 months, and lived in a home where there were many harsh rules and regulations, particularly around cleanliness and orderliness. She emerged into an anal character and became very orderly, frugal, and parsimonious. These traits were a defense against her wish to "shit and piss all over the place"—a wish which became activated during sex with a man, but which had to be repressed. Like many individuals, Jessica had associated excretion with sexuality and believed sex was a form of evacuation.

Inasmuch as toilet-training is one of the first strong demands placed on a youngster, ambivalence is an inevitable response. How these conflicts are resolved will, in many ways, determine whether the individual will become a cooperative and happy marital partner, a defiant, rebellious and obstinate mate, or an inhibited, unattached person.

Regression and Fixation

To better understand how psychosexual growth influences the adult's interpersonal relationships, the concepts of regression and fixation are quite pertinent. By regression we mean a retreat to an earlier phase of libidinal and/or ego organization. For example, a child under the impact of anxiety induced at toilet-training might regress to oral preoccupations and resume thumb-sucking. As an adult, feeling anxiety because of the demands of a situation or a relationship, the same individual may retreat from the situation or relationship and regress to overeating or excessive and compulsive dieting.

When unresolved conflicts and anxieties from specific developmental phases impinge on the mental apparatus and create areas of weakness, we term this process *fixation*. It is as if remnants of functioning at a particular stage of development are fixed in the psyche, ready to play a significant role in a later situation (Moore and Fine 1990). An example of an oral fixation would be a child of 6 constantly sucking his thumb while clinging to a doll. An anal fixation might involve a 6-year-old, terrified of being toilet-trained, constantly wetting and messing her pants.

An alcoholic adult might suffer from oral regression or oral fixation. If he or she drinks when interpersonal demands become too great and anxiety erupts, this is a regression. However, if the person has been depressed most of his or her life and has had little to do with people because of a strong distrust of them, we may view this kind of behavior as an oral fixation.

The Phallic-Oedipal Stage (Initiative vs Guilt)

Until the age of about 3, children love both parents indiscriminately. However, usually between 3 and 4, youngsters turn their affection more to the parent of the opposite sex and compete with the parent of the same sex (Freud 1905). The anthropologist Malinowski (1922) studied family patterns in several cultures and concluded that the oedipal conflict (frequently referred to as "the family romance") is a universal phenomenon.

The oedipal conflict is experienced differently by each of the sexes. With regard to the boy, from birth he is primarily dependent on his mother for comfort and security and continues to value her as a source of sustenance. However, by the time he is 3, he begins to feel romantic as well as loving toward her. As he observes his father romancing his mother, the boy wants to do the same. He competes with his father and begins to experience him as a dangerous rival for his mother's affections. Because of the boy's competitive fantasies toward his father, he fears his father's anger, disapproval, and retaliation.

From dreams and fantasies of children and adults, it is quite clear that the boy unconsciously fears that his father will maim and castrate him for his oedipal desires. Yet, because the boy needs and loves his father, he frequently feels guilty for wishing to hurt him and displace him. Quite frequently, if not always, out of fear of father's revenge the boy submits to father and becomes very compliant toward him.

Many of the interpersonal problems of unattached men emanate from their unresolved oedipal conflicts. Some men experience a woman's positive response to them as a hostile triumph over other men, feel guilty for their victory, and cannot permit the relationship with the woman to endure.

Ken, age 37, was in intensive therapy because he could not sustain a relationship with a woman. Although he had no difficulty meeting women and having them fall in love with him, sooner or later he would find himself feeling "bored," "depressed," and "losing interest" in them.

As he explored his fantasies, dreams, and history with his female therapist, he learned that every involvement he had with a woman was an attempt to displace his father and/or father figures. His unhappy state of mind after "winning" a woman came from his self-inflicted punishment for believing he had hurt and displaced his father.

Inasmuch as men can unconsciously make women they value and love into mother figures, closeness to them, particularly sexual closeness, can feel like a dangerous act of incest. When men turn closeness to women into forbidden incest, they can become impotent and defend themselves against all forms of intimacy. Often, they can only be sexually potent with women they do not value.

Larry, age 45, sought psychotherapy because "over and over again," he became sexually impotent with the women he loved. He was able to feel much more relaxed both sexually and emotionally with those women with whom he did not feel particularly tender. He divided women into two camps—those who were "nice" and "could be brought home to Mama," and those "who liked to fuck."

He could not fuse tender and erotic impulses toward the same woman because that would make him "feel like a motherfucker." As he learned to accept his sexual fantasies toward his mother and allow her to be a sexual person, he could become more relaxed with women.

When men feel very guilty toward their fathers for wanting to displace them (or believe they already have), they may avoid women altogether. Many of these men spend their time exclusively with males and/or become exclusively homosexual.

> Malcolm, age 40, was referred to a family agency to help him cope better with his cocaine addiction. In working with his social worker, a woman, he told her that he would do better talking things over with a man. Exploration of his wish to have a male therapist brought out that Malcolm was very close to his mother as a boy and feared his father. Because he was intimidated by his father and feared retaliation for feeling so loving toward his mother, Malcolm stayed with men and had little to do with women.

Although the girl's oedipal conflict has many similarities to that of the boy, there is one major difference. The girl becomes a rival of the parent who has been her main emotional provider. Consequently, she is caught in a powerful dilemma: whether to relinquish the dependency on her mother which has been gratifying and necessary, or try to maintain it while risking its disruption as she pursues father. Many women as adults cannot pursue relationships with men because they feel their relationship with their mother will be in jeopardy.

> Nancy was a very attractive professional woman in her middle fifties. Despite the fact that she had a great deal going for her—looks, intelligence, a successful career—she failed miserably in her relationships with men. Often she dated married men who were ambivalent about their marriages. However, she never succeeded in persuading them to leave their wives.

As her therapy unfolded, it became clear that succeeding in a relationship with a man was equivalent to taking her father away from her mother. This was an intriguing and exciting idea, but it filled her with enormous guilt.

Although very competitive with her mother, Nancy was very attached to her as well. To move toward a man and love him, as she experienced it, was undoing her attachment to her mother—an exciting possibility but something that felt "too criminal."

When women, like their male counterparts, turn their partners into parental figures, they feel ashamed of their incestuous fantasies. Thus they have to inhibit themselves sexually and emotionally with their mates whom they have made into father figures.

Olive, a woman in her late 30s, had a history of relationships with men in which she was constantly abused, physically and emotionally.

In her therapy in a mental health clinic, she discovered that her involvement with rejecting and abusive men was an unconscious attempt to deprive herself of sexual and emotional pleasure. If she enjoyed herself with her male partners, she felt as if she was "abusing" her father. She realized after a year of treatment that she would rather be punished and abused than feel "dirty" and "abusive."

Sometimes when a girl has idealized her father and feels that no man can surpass him, she unconsciously rejects every man she meets. Men who have idealized their mothers do the same thing with women—they reject them, thus preserving the idealized relationship with the mother.

Many women who seek psychotherapy have had fathers who subtly arranged for their daughters to love only them, and therefore try to prevent their daughters from moving away from them. Eventually, the daughter internalizes her father's admonitions, rejecting men in order to comply with her father's wishes.

> Penny, a woman in her middle forties, reported to her therapist that after dating men a few times, she would find herself finding fault with them. As her therapist listened to her criticisms of her partners, it became clear that she was constantly comparing the men she dated with the image of her father. Over and over again she had to demean the men so that she could maintain her secret love affair with her father.

One of the universal characteristics of children is that they have omnipotent fantasies and want their wishes gratified instantly. Children, in effect, want everything in sight. All boys want to give birth to babies and fantasize having breasts and vaginas. Similarly, when girls turn toward their fathers, they want to own his penis. Since this is not possible, they may try to grab the penis and the power they ascribe to it from the men they date. This eventually alienates them from men.

> Rita, in her late twenties, sought therapy because she found herself in constant bitter feuds with the men she dated. In her therapy, which was intensive analysis, she

was able to uncover fantasies and dreams of biting off men's penises and keeping them for herself. As she got in touch with how much she devaluated herself as a woman and overvalued men and "their powerful penises," she could begin to accept herself more as a woman with a vagina she could like and enjoy.

According to Erikson (1950), the maturational dilemma to be resolved in the oedipal period for all children is that of taking initiative vs feeling guilty. Boys and girls who feel very guilty about their oedipal fantasies can become docile, passive, and unassertive. However, if the oedipal period has been relatively free of conflict, the youngster will enrich his or her capacity to achieve and to love. Such a child will be able to form an enjoyable, trusting attachment as a carryover from the trust—mistrust stage (oral period), to be cooperative and yet feel autonomous because the anal stage was successful, and to admire the loved person of the opposite sex and take initiative with the partner.

The Latency Stage (Industry vs Inferiority)

If youngsters have resolved most of their oedipal conflicts, they are able to move from their families to the social world of their peers. Although children still need security and comfort from their families, by the time they are 6 or 7 years of age they should be increasingly able to forgo some childish pleasures and begin to empathize with the wishes of others. The period from age 6 to 10 has been called the latency period because the intensity of the youngster's instinctual impulses, that is, sexual and aggressive drives, is temporarily subdued. It is during this time that children attempt to give up their romantic attachments to the parent of the opposite sex and to reduce their competition with the same-sex parent. Roheim (1952), an anthropologist, has concluded that the degree of renouncement of romantic preoccupation during the latency period depends a great deal on the climate of the particular culture in which the child is being socialized. Thus, the degree of sexual preoccupation in latency varies widely.

Fine (1975) has demonstrated that early in the latency period children have their first love affair with a youngster of the opposite sex. This is observed in most children and is recalled by most adults. Because the child cannot easily give up the attachment to the parent of the opposite sex, he or she needs a substitute. A child who does not have a first love affair with a peer during early latency has not succeeded in being liberated from his or her parents.

During the latter half of the latency period, many children confine themselves to the same-sex groups and often express a great deal of contempt toward members of the opposite sex. Rather than acknowledge the sexual attraction that might reactivate oedipal conflicts, children defend themselves by denying love and expressing hatred; they use the defense of reaction formation, expressing only one side of their ambivalence and denying the other part.

Many unattached men and women who have not resolved oedipal conflicts behave like latency children. They avoid one-to-one relationships with the opposite sex and spend more time in groups with members of their own sex. Often they denounce members of the opposite sex.

> Sam, a man of 29, was referred for psychotherapy to a community mental health clinic by a court because of antisocial behavior while under the influence of alcohol. In his therapy sessions with a male clinician, he constantly denounced women and spoke warmly of his male confreres with whom he spent almost all of his free time.
>
> In reviewing his childhood, Sam was able to recall how often his mother paraded in the nude, was very seductive with him, and tried to make him into a quasi-lover. Sam, during his seventh month of twice-a-week therapy declared, "I felt my mother was trying to get me in the sack and I ran like hell. Being with guys is better."

> Terry, in her late forties, was a lesbian who came to treatment because her female lover had broken up with her. In reviewing her history, Terry told her therapist that she always felt under scrutiny by her "voyeuristic" father. She claimed that he never let her alone and was often busy trying to fondle her. To escape from her father's sexual advances and the anxiety it induced, Terry renounced men.

How well children cope with latency issues is an excellent way of determining how they will deal in serious relationships with members of the opposite sex. The latency child who enters school, similar to the adult who

enters an intimate relationship, must share more than he
or she did previously. He or she can no longer be
exclusively narcissistic. When children enter school, they
need to develop empathy, mutuality, and be able to
compromise, negotiate, and take on frustration. This is
also required of men and women who wish to attach to
members of the opposite sex. If they have resolved the
issues of the latency period, tamed their egoistic concerns,
and mastered their oedipal conflicts, they are usually
capable of a close attachment to a member of the opposite
sex.

Many unattached adults handle their problems and
frustrations in a manner similar to the way latency children deal with infantile wishes—by projecting their immature desires onto the opposite sex. Many unattached men
and women criticize members of the opposite sex as
immature, unkind, self-involved, and so forth, not realizing that they themselves are behaving unkindly and
immaturely. A favorite pastime of latency children is
tattling on their peers. Similarly, many single men and
women love to gossip and demean members of the
opposite sex—often projecting onto their counterparts
difficulties of their own.

> Upton, a 50-year-old confirmed bachelor, was in treatment
> because of a severe depression after a close male friend
> was diagnosed with AIDS. In his therapy he did not talk
> much about his friend. Instead, he criticized many women
> he had met who were "too morose, too depressed, and too
> critical."

Erikson (1950) suggested that the task of the latency period is to resolve the conflict between "industry and inferiority." Men and women who have resolved the tasks of this stage of development usually feel confident of their inner resources. With a good sense of self-esteem, they are free to love and enjoy partners of the opposite sex.

Adolescence (Identity vs Identity Diffusion)

Although there is variation from culture to culture, adolescence is usually a turbulent time—a time of much conflict. As biological growth takes place and teenagers become capable of a full sex life, many of their elders want to curb their sexual outlets. And although teenagers want to be treated as independent adults, they also retain a yearning for parental nurturance and direction. What is most characteristic of adolescents in most cultures is ambivalence. Teenagers want independence, yet they fear it. They have strong desires to be given to, yet feel very embarrassed by their dependent cravings. They want sexual contact but often feel ashamed of their sexual fantasies. They aspire to greatness but feel apprehensive about surpassing their parents and other parental figures.

Those clinicians who have studied teenagers have noted the adolescents' strong propensity to recapitulate their complete psychosexual development during this time and to reexperience old conflicts (Blos 1967, Esman 1979, A. Freud 1958). Oral conflicts manifest themselves in the teenagers' peculiar food habits. Adolescents can be very symbiotic one day and reclusive the next. Their conflicts with anality are apparent in their desire to be rebellious, obstinate, and preoccupied with "dirty" jokes and "dirty" clothes and rooms. They can move from promiscuity to celibacy within a few days as they struggle with revived oedipal conflicts. They can deride success and achievement one day and become super-ambitious the next.

If the adolescent does not establish a cohesive identity and become comfortable with her role in work and love, he or she will be inclined to form a turbulent, unhappy, ambivalent relationship with a prospective marital partner. Many unattached men and women feel half adult and half child, guilty about sexuality, terrified of autonomy, and overwhelmed by dependency. Instead of feeling intimate with a partner, they isolate themselves.

> Victoria, age 23, sought help at a college counseling center. Every time she was involved in a serious relationship with a young man, she became very nauseated, could not sleep, needed all kinds of reassurance from her women friends, and was unable to concentrate on her studies.
>
> In her treatment sessions she was able to learn that ever since her early adolescence, a big part of her was rejecting all forms of sexuality. Her adolescence reactivated acute problems on all levels of development. She recalled having a depressed mother during infancy, harsh toilet-training later, and an overstimulating father during her oedipal stage of development. All of these conflicts interfered with her ability to enjoy a warm, intimate relationship with a man.

It is important for a therapist to recognize that every individual recapitulates his or her unique psychosexual development when he or she enters or tries to enter a love relationship with a member of the opposite sex. In effect, each individual follows an inner script based on his or her life story. If the man or woman has successfully resolved problems at each level of development and mastered the tasks such as trust vs mistrust, autonomy vs shame and doubt, he or she is psychologically prepared to enter into and enjoy a mature, loving relationship.

Because many individuals, married and unmarried, have not been helped to resolve conflicts at various stages of development, they love in an immature fashion. The following are immature forms of love that we frequently observe in our unattached patients.

Immature Forms of Love

Immature forms of love are not chosen in a deliberate, conscious manner (Fine 1975). As Bergler (1963) has suggested, the human psyche is formed early in childhood and the result is enshrined in the person, usually without his or her awareness. A love relationship, he notes, does not create anything new in the partners—their wishes, defenses, and coping mechanisms existed long before the partners met. There are few, if any, innocent victims of interpersonal discord; their misfortunes have been unconsciously arranged by themselves.

Celibate Love

The celibate man or woman is usually very frightened of and guilty about his or her erotic wishes. Unable to fuse tender and erotic feelings, this person often loves an institution such as a church or political organization rather then another individual. Concomitantly he or she renounces overt sexuality. Celibate men and women frequently have been unable to master and monitor sexual feelings toward parental figures. Thus, they have an unconscious tendency to turn their partners into parents and then feel very uncomfortable about reactivated incestuous and oedipal conflicts. These people can love but cannot enjoy sex.

Clinging Love

Here, the individual is almost always submissive and is ready to renounce everything for the loved partner. Lacking a sense of identity and having limited self-esteem and self-confidence, the clinging person is ingratiating, flattering, and never feels worthy. Although able to attract a partner who enjoys being constantly praised, the clinger rarely gratifies his or her wish to have an omnipotent and always available parent. Further, the clinger's partner soon or later feels contemptuous of the mate's self-demeaning behavior and the relationship usually ends fairly soon. The clinger usually has not enjoyed "a good enough mother" one who offers "a holding environment" that provides an optimal amount of constancy and comfort for the growing child (Winnicott 1971).

Compulsive Love

This form of love is an attempt to defend against all kinds of self-doubts and anxieties. For example, by having compulsive sex with a member of the opposite sex, the compulsive lover can deny homosexual urges which create anxiety and self-doubt. Or, by declaring their love to their partners incessantly, compulsive lovers can deny their hatred. By involving themselves in a relationship in which they receive constant attention from the mate, they can reaffirm their shaky self-images and low self-esteem.

The compulsive lover rarely derives much pleasure from love relationships because the psychosexual conflicts that are the basis of this love are never resolved.

Critical Love

The critical partner usually finds a guilt-ridden mate who feels a strong need to be punished for real or imagined sins. In critical love, the critic seizes upon a quality in the partner that she cannot tolerate within herself. Instead of facing their own unacceptable wishes, defenses, or character traits, critical lovers project their problems onto the partner and demean them. Critical lovers tell us a great deal about themselves when they blast their partners for their poor eating habits, sloppy dress, unsexy behavior, and so forth. They tell us about their own problems.

Homosexual Love

During the last two decades, homosexual love has been a controversial issue even among psychodynamic theorists and clinicians. Although Freud viewed homosexuality as a regression and maladaptation (1905), modern psychodynamic literature (for example, Fogel et al. 1986), views homosexuality as a biological given with different societies and cultures taking different views of it, more often with a critical and pejorative stance.

Many clinicians who have worked intensively with homosexual men and women have noted that almost all of them had had very frustrating childhoods (Fine 1988, Socarides 1978). Having experienced poor role models who failed to demonstrate that love between members of opposite sexes can be enjoyable and enriching, homosexual men and women are frequently coping with much rage, even though much of their rage is unconscious.

In any discussion of homosexuality, we have to differentiate between homosexuality as a life-style, a civil rights issue, and a psychosocial problem (Strean 1984). As a lifestyle, homosexuality has been acclaimed and defamed over the centuries. More recently homosexuals have been beginning to attain what they rightly deserve—equal protection under the law and the right to enjoy without discrimination all the privileges and rights that all citizens have.

Homosexuals have to cope with all the hatred that has been misdirected at them by those who have not accepted that homosexuality is something in all of us. In addition, homosexuals frequently have unresolved developmental problems, particularly at the oedipal level. Like many compulsive heterosexual lovers who have to deny their unacceptable homosexual wishes, homosexuals are often compelled to seek out members of their own gender because their heterosexual feelings and fantasies create intense anxiety for them.

In *Being Homosexual: Gay Men and Their Development*, psychoanalyst Richard Isay (1989), presents his conviction that sexual orientation, whether it be homosexual, heterosexual, or bisexual, "is constitutionally set and immutable from birth" (p. 2). Furthermore, he has found no differences in the parenting of gay men as compared with heterosexual men. Therefore, he concludes that a genetic factor is responsible for sexual orientation.

Arguing for a more neutral attitude toward homosexuality and not seeing it as a perversion, another psychoanalyst, Richard Friedman (1988) in *Male Homosexuality: A Contemporary Psychoanalytic Perspective*, feels that psychoanalysts have been too rigid in their diagnostic appraisals of homosexual patients. Friedman states:

> There is no homosexual or heterosexual character type. In fact, it would appear that homosexuality,

bisexuality, and heterosexuality are distributed across the entire range of character types and character structures. [p. 81]

Loving the Partner's Parents

An underestimated factor in immature love is the possibility of falling in love with the partner's parents. The individual, in looking for a new family with better parents than he or she had, relates much more to the mate's parents than to the mate. The latter eventually feels ignored and the relationship deteriorates.

Masochistic Love

The masochistic lover is full of self-hate and is a very guilt-ridden person. Attracted to a powerful person who punishes him, the masochist derives unconscious gratification in being demeaned and devalued. Being loved by a powerful person seems more important to the masochist than feeling self-respect.

Inasmuch as masochistic individuals have feared asserting themselves with their strict parents, their vengeance goes underground; instead of permitting themselves to voice their anger, they feel guilty for just feeling it. They flagellate themselves, thinking that if they continually cry "mea culpa," their punitive mates will finally love them.

According to Theodor Reik in *Masochism in Modern Man* (1941), masochistic individuals rarely suffer alone. Most of the time their chief witnesses are their mates. The lamb-skin they wear hides a wolf. Their yielding always includes defiance. Their compliance always contains opposition.

What is extremely important to keep in mind about masochistic behavior is that it protects the individual from fantasied danger. The danger that the masochist frequently worries about is acting out repressed sadism (Strean 1994).

Rescuing Love

Rescuing love, although observed in both sexes, is more often found among men. The rescuer wishes to save a woman from her unhappy lot and tries to strengthen her through his ministrations. This behavior seems to derive from the boy's wish to perceive his mother as the unhappy victim of his father's domination; that is, she was forced to have sex with father. Many boys, in their competition with their fathers, like to feel that father is abusing mother sexually so that they can have a reason to save and possess her. This belief is often played out in the fantasy of many boys and men who imagine themselves rescuing a whore from other males who exploit her (Fine 1975).

As in all forms of immature love, the rescuer, whether it be a man or woman, rarely sustains the enjoyment of the relationship. Inasmuch as the rescuer is unconsciously rescuing a parental figure, he or she begins to feel guilty and then turns off sexually and interpersonally, or finds ways to punish himself or herself for fantasied transgressions. The unhappy man or woman who was rescued begins to feel betrayed by the partner's withdrawal and after a while does not feel rescued at all.

Revengeful Love

When an individual has been abused by his or her family, he or she will seek revenge. Men and women who want to avenge hurts may seek a partner who will upset their parents and/or other family members. If family members have certain intellectual, political, or religious values which are important to them, the person who seeks revenge may unconsciously choose a partner whose values are an antithesis to the family in order to enjoy their discomfort.

Sadistic Love

Sadistic individuals usually feel very weak but compensate for their vulnerability by finding a lover whom they can derogate and demean. Sadistic men and women tend to place their partners in the position they most fear—a position of weakness. They try to humiliate their partners in the way they were humiliated.

A sadist almost always chooses and identifies with a masochistic mate and the masochistic mate usually selects a sadistic partner. When the sadistic partner begins to feel guilty for his or her belligerent behavior and/or the masochistic mate begins to feel rage after being demeaned incessantly, the partners often switch roles with the masochist becoming the sadist and vice versa.

Unrequited Love

For some individuals the more unavailable and unattainable the love object, the more lovable the object becomes. Because these men and women have a strong tendency to turn the love object into a parental figure who is considered perfect, actually to be attached to the much admired person feels too much like forbidden incest. Unrequited lovers can feel passion but only from afar. Like all immature lovers, they cannot fuse tender and erotic feelings and love one person consistently and pleasurably.

Narcissistic Love

With the advent of self psychology (Kohut 1971, 1977), narcissistic love has been a helpful concept in describing those who cannot sustain loving attachments. In narcissistic love, the man or woman must have the focus of attention constantly. He or she feels very vulnerable and desperate if not fully acknowledged, and usually experiences overwhelming rage when frustrated by a lack of appreciation. In the therapy situation, the narcissistic patient makes constant demands on the therapist for recognition, admiration, and praise. This is referred to as "the mirror transference" (Kohut 1977).

Falling in Love vs Loving

Many unattached men and women can fall in love but cannot participate in sustained loving. It is useful to differentiate between the two emotional states.

Falling in love has many unrealistic qualities and is obsessional and egocentric. Freud (1939) likened romantic lovers to fond parents who project their own ideal onto their child in order to substitute for the lost narcissism of their own childhoods. He pointed out that what the lover wishes he or she could have been, is fantasized for the beloved. Freud concluded that falling in love is an irrational, immature, and unrealistic response based on the reawakening of family romances of childhood.

In the "honeymoon" stage of a romance, the lover, having overidealized the partner, is emotionally convinced that the best person on earth has been found and that together they have found Paradise. The lover lives only for giving to his beloved because he or she believes that the partner is doing the very same thing (Ables 1977). The essence of falling in love is exclusivity—the feeling that one is fulfilling the partner's needs so completely that he or she does not and could not have any interest in anyone else (Freud 1914).

Romantic love can never endure indefinitely because reality asserts itself and lovers begin to realize that they cannot depend on each other for everything. As a man and woman begin to perceive each other's real characteristics, an inevitable disillusionment occurs. The romantic ideal in retrospect was a fantasy and they resent each other for being imperfect humans. From a psychodynamic perspective, the myth that romantic love can endure forever emanates from a fantasy that there really is an omnipotent, perfect parent somewhere who can supply eternal bliss.

In his paper on narcissism, Freud (1914) concluded that

the choice of a love object is either anaclitically or narcis-sistically based. The individual who makes an anaclitic choice is oriented primarily toward nurturance and pro-tection and is focused primarily on gratifying dependency wishes. A narcissistic choice is made by a person who sees himself or herself as the object. The individual who is chosen either represents the ideal self or a projected ego ideal. Inasmuch as the choice of a love object is based on irrational childish wishes, a love object can never provide full gratification for too long. As mentioned earlier in this chapter, Kohut (1971, 1977) has enlarged our under-standing of narcissism.

Loving, in contrast to "falling in love," is based on reality and accepts the fact that the beloved is a human being with limitations who cannot consistently gratify childish fantasies. Mature love necessitates mutuality. This implies that both individuals can enjoy giving to and taking from the other within a trusting relationship. Both grant each other autonomy without either partner feeling hostile or threatened about it. Loving maturely, as we have reiterated, also implies a fusion of tender and erotic wishes for both partners. This suggests that both partners can monitor their narcissism, tame childish wishes, and not parentify each other too much.

Although the mature person should be able to give and take love, identify with the partner's needs, and enjoy his counterpart's doing likewise, he is able to have enough of a self-image and sufficient autonomy that the lack of love at a particular time or the lack of validation at another time, does not destroy.

Enjoying a wide range of feelings, the mature person

knows when to defer gratification. He can trust his environment where it can be trusted and knows when to be cautious. Maturity, as has been implied, involves the capacity to be relatively autonomous, to feel independent without resenting or feeling shameful or doubtful about one's strengths. Loving individuals can enjoy their sexual roles and take initiative as men or women without worrying that they are supplanting someone else.

Fine, who has written a great deal about mature love (1975, 1985), suggests that just as the emotionally healthy child in growing up moves from *attachment* to the mother to *admiration* of both parents, followed by *sexual enjoyment* in adolescence, which leads to an *intimate* relationship with one person of the opposite sex, followed by *devotion* to children, the loving and mature adult should feel and demonstrate these five aspects in a love relationship with a mate.

It is the thesis of this book that if an individual has resolved childhood conflicts and is not bombarded by childish fantasies, he or she will marry so that he or she can love and be loved in a trusting, tender, and sexually gratifying relationship. Those who rebel against marriage or cannot achieve it, such as the unattached who are the focus of this book, are frequently unhappy people who tend to rationalize their complaints and problems. They are usually uninformed about the psychological forces that make them unhappy. Most often, they need psychotherapy so that they can mature and lead more pleasureful and fulfilling lives.

3

Therapeutic Principles in Treating the Unattached Patient

In order to help any individual in psychotherapy, certain processes and procedures are essential regardless of the setting or the patient. Some of these processes and procedures are gathering data, planning treatment, choosing a treatment modality (for example, couples counseling, brief treatment, group therapy) and selecting specific interventive procedures at critical times such as interpretation, clarification, or confrontation.

Of crucial importance in any psychotherapeutic encounter is individualizing the patient. All patients must be viewed as unique and should feel that the therapist regards them as special.

In this chapter I will discuss some of the important

principles in treating the unattached patient. Although the principles I stress may also be applicable to other groups of patients, they have been used successfully by many therapists for many years in their treatment of the unattached patient.

Initial Interviews

A constant finding by psychotherapy researchers is that close to half of the individuals who seek therapeutic help leave treatment prematurely (Strean 1985). Many reasons have been offered to try to explain this phenomenon, such as poor motivation and severe pathology of the patient, the therapist's lack of sufficient training, an absence of rapport between patient and therapist, unresolvable resistances of the patient and unresolvable counterresistances of the therapist.

One factor that has not been sufficiently considered in patient dropout that applies particularly to therapeutic work with the unattached is that too many clinicians talk too much and do not listen enough. Individuals who seek psychotherapy have usually discussed their problems with others, only to find that they are quick to give advice, change the subject, and end up discussing their own agendas. Individuals in conflict need something better.

The Importance of Listening

What all patients want and what unattached patients desperately need is somebody to listen to them and not bombard them with many questions, lengthy comments, unsolicited advice, and frequent interpretations. As mentioned in Chapter 2, unattached people have often felt misunderstood and mistreated because they were insufficiently individualized and not sufficiently empathized with in their formative years. Often they are unattached because a close relationship with another human being has been and still is quite threatening. Hence, the therapist who works with unattached men and women must help these threatened and cynical individuals slowly to feel safe enough to reveal their anxieties, conflicts, and terrors in an atmosphere that is non-judgmental, caring, and not overwhelming.

It takes clinicians a long time to convince themselves that a good interviewer is a good listener. They learn that the patients who stay in treatment are those who have been given many opportunities to have a concerned listener attend empathetically to their feelings, thoughts, and memories. Clinicians who have had considerable therapeutic experience with the unattached know that what helps these patients most is pouring their hearts out to somebody who listens quietly with concern and compassion. Throughout the treatment process and particularly in the initial interviews, if most of the time is spent with the patient talking while the therapist listens, many wonderful results can eventuate. Patients' tensions are reduced, their thoughts become clarified, their self-esteem rises as they feel understood by their therapists. Energy previously tied up in defending themselves becomes more available for pleasureful interaction with others.

Begin at the Beginning

An old axiom of casework and psychotherapy is "begin where the client is" (Garrett 1951, Kadushin 1972, Strean 1978). If clients and patients, particularly those who are unattached, are to feel free to be themselves and expose their hurts, angers, vulnerabilities, guilts, and humiliations to the clinician, they have to feel convinced that what is of concern to them at the moment is what the therapist most wants to hear. One of the major problems of unattached men and women is they have frequently experienced parental figures, siblings, and others as individuals who have been and are overly concerned with their own wishes and not emotionally available to them. The unattached tend to carry this conviction into all their relationships and have a tendency to shy away from others in order to protect themselves from humiliating rejection. Consequently, they very much need a therapist who shows them from the start that the patient's concerns are always the number one priority.

Particularly in the first interviews, therapists tend to be too compulsive about their own agendas. Many, for example, are too eager to announce their fee policy while the patient wants to discuss current aches and pains. These therapists apparently do not recognize that the establishment of a fee might be more palatable to the patient after, not before, he or she has discussed with the therapist hurts and worries and has observed the therapist to be a good listener.

In the initial interviews, many therapists show their compulsiveness by routinely asking questions about the patient's history when the patient may want to discuss, for example, his or her current sense of isolation. Another grievous therapeutic error in the initial interviews with the unattached is announcing the ground rules of treatment, for example: punctuality, no major life decisions during the course of therapy, discouragement of absences and payment for same, and so forth. The reason this procedure is particularly contraindicated for unattached patients is that they have frequently been subjected in their pasts to arbitrary and insensitive discipline. Thus, they frequently rebel against all kinds of limits and controls, feeling they are being imposed upon—not for their own benefit, but for the benefit of those who impose the limits. Consequently, it behooves the therapist with the unattached to wait until the patient is absent or late a couple of times (if, indeed, he or she ever will be), before discussing "the rules" that govern the therapy.

Initial Resistances

Inasmuch as unattached patients tend to be very uncomfortable and suspicious in close, intimate relationships, they have more than the usual ambivalence about getting involved in treatment. They may feel very anxious about revealing their emotional, sexual, and interpersonal difficulties; they may worry about being judged, unloved, or rejected by the therapist. They are frequently concerned about being accused, blamed, or criticized; they often fear that their situation will be labeled as hopeless, and occasionally they are apprehensive about therapy making them worse.

All of the aforementioned issues may not be directly discussed in the initial interviews by the prospective patients. Instead, they may try to get the therapist to prove that he or she will definitely help ease their ills. Or, the patient may try to get the therapist to explain how therapy will work. Sometimes the unattached person tries to draw the clinician into an argument. Or, ask for some advice. Or, beg to be reassured. Or, question the therapist's qualifications. Or, try some other means to defeat the idea of beginning treatment. There are several pitfalls that the therapist who wants to work with the unattached should try to avoid, particularly in the early phases of treatment. Let's consider some of them.

The Inadvisability of Advice

In the initial phase of treatment, frequently in the first interview, the unattached man or woman may ask the therapist for advice. The patient may want to know if more attendance at parties for singles is advisable or may want advice on how to behave sexually. Often the prospective patient wants to know what to do about a romance that is failing or what to say or not to say to a significant other.

What is extremely important for therapists to remind themselves continually is that whenever patients ask for advice, they are in a state of uncertainty, ambivalence, and helplessness. They ask the therapist for advice because they are wrestling with a "yes" and a "no" about the subject under consideration. When patients are ambivalent about an issue and the therapist tells them what to do, nothing is really achieved because the ambivalence is not resolved. Either the patient will follow the therapist's orders or rebel against them, but how or why the patient cannot resolve the uncertainty is not faced. He or she remains helpless.

> In his first interview at a mental health clinic, Zave, age 36, asked his female interviewer if he should have sex with a woman on a first date. Not recognizing the implication of the question, that it was Zave's "first date" with the interviewer and he was probably reluctant to talk about his attraction to her, the therapist gave a quick response. She told Zave that most women were reluctant to go to bed on a first date.
>
> Although Zave nodded in assent, he never did return for a second interview.

Because the therapist did not take into consideration the burgeoning erotic transference that the patient was experiencing, she unwittingly arranged for him to feel rejected and leave treatment. Furthermore, Zave's own ambivalence was not confronted; the therapist behaved more like an expert on morals, that is, a punitive superego, and only succeeded in further isolating the patient.

When advice is solicited from the therapist, the clinician should recognize with the patient that the question being posed is a difficult one to answer and perhaps therapist and patient together can try to understand the difficulty.

> Yvette, a woman of 40, sought help from a therapist in private practice because her female lover wanted to break up. Yvette was very depressed at the possible loss but also angry and hurt about the position she felt she was "put in." Toward the end of her first interview, Yvette asked the male therapist, "Do you think I should try to get her to stay?" The therapist responded, "I can understand your questioning this possibility. You seem to have a lot of mixed feelings about what to do." Yvette told the therapist that she felt on a see-saw, going up and down in her attitude, and was in agony. If she could only decide one way or another, she'd feel better. The therapist suggested to Yvette that he'd like to try to help relieve her agony. In response, Yvette said that she felt mixed about many things in life, including the issue of her gender identity. She wasn't sure whether she wanted to be with women exclusively and realized that was one reason why she chose a male therapist.

Reassurance Is Rarely Reassuring

As the unattached man or woman discusses his or her lonely existence in the initial interviews, often appearing quite depressed while doing so, and revealing a tumultuous history in which the patient did not feel very loved, it is often tempting to reassure the patient.

Even though reassurance can reduce anxiety for a few moments or for an hour or a day, it usually backfires.

Particularly for the unattached man or woman who harbors much self-hate and limited trust of the environment, the reassurance is usually questioned eventually. The reason is that the unattached person, like all patients, has a lot of unconscious investment in maintaining the status quo. Although he or she may feel lonely, the unattached person feels even more discomfort in being attached. Despite the fact that the unattached may feel humiliated by their inability to enjoy close interpersonal contacts, they may be more overwhelmed in the face of them.

When the therapist reassures the patient that he or she will eventually get married or live with someone, have good sex soon, or something similar, the therapist is unwittingly manipulating the patient to travel in a direction that is too frightening.

> When Victor, a man in his early twenties, asked his therapist in his second interview if he would stop blushing on his dates with women, his male therapist responded, "Sure, as we talk about your problems, it will help you relax more." Although the therapist was correct in assuming that talking can lead to a diminution or even a cessation of symptoms, he did not investigate Victor's need for reassurance or what was happening to Victor internally. Victor left treatment after the fourth interview.

It is important to reiterate that when patients seek reassurance, they are feeling overwhelmed by many conflicts. What is crucial for the therapist to keep in mind is that patients will eventually welcome a full discussion of their inner states, even though it will involve considerable time and effort, and even some pain. They eventually welcome a full discussion of their problems because they soon realize that the therapist is being candid and, in addition, they really know within themselves that there is no simple solution to complex problems.

> Ursula, a woman in her thirties, told her female therapist that she was quite convinced that men did not want to date her because she was obese. When the therapist did not comment on this, Ursula queried, "Do you think that therapy will help me lose weight?" The therapist responded, "Eating food can serve many purposes. Perhaps we could discuss what you are feeling when you eat."
>
> Although Ursula appeared dumbfounded at first, she was able to involve herself in a series of discussions on her loneliness, her deep dependency wishes, and her anger. She learned that she relied on food much more than she did on people. As Ursula was able to rely on the therapist and discuss her aches and pains in a safe atmosphere, she did lose ten pounds. The real loss of weight was reassuring!

On Answering Questions

When prospective patients are being cared for, it is often a new experience for them and they begin to question whether the current positive experience can endure. Doubting the efficacy of the therapeutic process, wondering about the therapist's motives, and still worrying about exposing themselves, they begin to ask the therapist questions about the latter's life and/or his or her professional qualifications. Occasionally they ask for explanations on how therapy really works. From time to time in the early interviews, patients want to know what the therapist thinks about political issues, sports, or almost anything that involves people, their problems, and their interactions.

There has been much debate among clinicians on the appropriateness of answering patients' questions. Some clinicians believe it is arrogant and inhumane to refuse to answer questions. Many mental health professionals take the position that the patient has the "right to know" just what the therapist's qualifications are. A few contend that facts about the therapist and the therapeutic process must be presented.

After experimenting and debating this issue for many years as well as observing hundreds of therapist–patient interactions where the patient has posed questions to the therapist, I have concluded that answering the patient's questions rarely helps the patient and/or the therapeutic process. What it can do is help the therapist feel a temporary lessening of anxiety, but only temporarily.

I have learned that when patients ask the therapist questions they are usually experiencing some doubts about the therapist, the process, and/or about some issues in their lives. For example, when a patient asks if the therapist is married, divorced, a Freudian, or belongs to the American Psychological Association, the patient is questioning the therapist's emotional and intellectual ability to help. It may even be that he wants to prove that the therapist cannot help.

Because I strongly believe that behind every question there is a statement—one that implies that the patient has doubts about the therapy and the therapist—I believe that getting the doubts out in the open should be the therapist's major task and major priority. Furthermore, it is important for every therapist to keep constantly in mind that the major purpose of therapy is to help patients understand themselves better. Self-understanding evolves when the patient's thoughts, wishes, fantasies, dreams, and history are explored and eventually understood. Answering a patient's questions may gratify her curiosity for awhile or lessen tension for a moment. It will rarely promote self-understanding or better mastery of her life.

When a patient asks the therapist a question, if the therapist genuinely believes the question is a product of the patient's uncertain feelings and anxieties, it then behooves the therapist to explore tactfully what the patient is feeling currently that prompts the question. This does not mean that the therapist coldly and mechanically queries, "Why do you ask?" It does mean that the therapist may say, "I can answer your question about (for example, my age, whether I'm married, if I'm a Freudian, or belong to the A.P.A.) but let's see if we can understand what you are feeling right now that prompts your question. I think that will help you more."

Though many, if not most, patients can cooperate with the therapist's wish to promote self-understanding, and will begin to explore their own motives for asking a question, some feel frustrated when not immediately gratified and cope with the frustration by becoming angry.

I believe it is to avoid the patient's verbalization of anger and to avoid frustrating him that therapists answer questions rather than subject the questions and motives to investigation. What the therapists fail to appreciate is that the patient's anger will not go away because his or her doubts about the issue still remain.

Patients' doubts and resistances to treatment endure throughout treatment (Strean 1990). Therefore, patients will always ask questions of their therapists. If therapists accept this notion as a fact of therapeutic life and really want to help patients understand their doubts and master their anxieties when questions are asked, they will explore their patients' feeling rather than answer them.

After over forty years of practice, I have come to a firm conviction that the patient is almost always questioning the therapist's intentions, motives, and good faith. I observed that when I first entered practice, patients questioned my youthful appearance. Now they wonder about my gray hair and if I'm sufficiently stable and healthy, that is, young enough, to help them. Like all clinicians, I attempted to answer questions about myself only to find out that I wasn't helping my patients. Even though I was trying to help myself when I answered questions, it never eased me.

The following are two clinical examples that demonstrate a way of dealing with the patient's questions in a compassionate and helpful matter, but without answering them.

> Tom, a single man in his forties, applied to a family agency for help and was assigned to a young female social worker

in her middle twenties. Toward the end of his first interview with the social worker, Tom remarked, "I liked our
chat, but tell me, are you practicing very long?" The social
worker responded, "Although you liked our chat, I think
you are worried that I may not have had enough experience to help you." Said Tom, "Touché! You may not have
had a lot of experience but you sure as hell know how to
deal with a guy's doubts. Yes, I do wonder about your age.
You are young enough to be my daughter!" The social
worker than asked, "Do you think as your daughter I
might not be able to help you? Maybe you think daughters
can't help fathers?"

In dealing with a patient's questions, the therapist, as in
the above vignette, must be able to empathize with the
patient's concerns and, to some extent, identify with
them. In addition, the practitioner, as was also true in the
above case, must remain non-defensive and non-wordy.

Sarah, age 35, sought help because she had just been
through a painful divorce. In her second interview she
asked her female therapist who was about her own age,
whether she was married. The therapist, not answering
the question directly, remarked, "After having had a
difficult marriage, are you wondering whether I am capable of knowing what marriage is like?"
Although Sarah was silent for a few moments, she went
on to say, "I'm not sure whether I'm against marriage in
general or not. If you are married, maybe you are my
enemy. Then again, if you are not married, maybe you'll
never help me become married again."
When she did not answer Sarah's question, the therapist was able to see how very ambivalent the patient was

about marriage, remarriage, and the helping process. Respecting her patient's ambivalence, the therapist stated, "I guess at this point it's difficult to know what you want of me—to be married, divorced, or unmarried—because you are not certain now what you'd like for yourself." Sarah responded, "I may not be sure I know what I want these days, but I like your candor."

In learning theory, there is an important principle called "the law of primacy" (Hall and Lindzey 1957). According to the law of primacy, we remember much better what we are exposed to first than what we are taught later. Hence, we will remember with more certainty our first day in school, our first date, our first patient, than those which follow. First impressions, in effect, often tend to be lasting ones.

The first interview in therapy, therefore, is probably one of the most, if not the most, important interview in therapy. If the patient is listened to very carefully, if the therapist does not talk too much, if the patient's doubts are explored, and the therapist respects the patient's resistance, the therapy is off to a good start. Thus, questions should not be quickly answered, reassurance not easily given, and the client listened to with what psychologist Carl Rogers (1951) has called "an unconditional positive regard."

The Presenting Problem

When unattached men and women seek counseling or psychotherapy, they are rarely clear about why they have sought help, or what exactly they want from the therapy. Often they are vague about their problems, embarrassed in presenting them, and have to conceal, especially in the initial interviews, what ails them.

It is very important for the therapist not to take the prospective patient's requests too literally because, similar to dreams, their manifest content masks their real meaning. For example, when a prospective patient says that he's come for help to break up with his girlfriend, exploring his request might yield that the uninitiated patient may feel very ambivalent about his relationship with his girlfriend and does not really know what he wants to do. Or, the divorced wife who comes to a family agency or mental health clinic to get some help to force her ex-husband to adhere to visitation agreements, and upon exploration of her request, therapist and client may learn that she has some hidden wishes that she is fighting, to reconcile with her husband.

When therapists do not take their patients' presenting problems and/or presenting requests literally, they can enter into their patients' world and help them talk. In this way, not only are latent wishes and conflicts better clarified, but patients often feel less tension with more energy available to explore further hidden facets of the problems that brought them to the initial interview.

Although the competent therapist is one who is always alert for hidden motives and latent conflicts, he does not reject the prospective patient's presentation by telling her that the real problem is something else. Rather, the therapist explores further the patient's presentation and its implied requests.

Over forty years ago, social work educator Gordon Hamilton (1951) pointed out that at intake every request by the client reflects a need which has to be understood. The request, no matter how farfetched, needs to be heard in all of its details and explored in depth. Hamilton concluded that what the client presents and how it is presented always needs to be respected by the practitioner.

> Ralph, a man in his late twenties, came to a private practitioner for "help in locating a wife." He told his interviewer early in the consultation that therapists had lots of people in their practices who were single; therefore Ralph was quite sure the therapist could introduce him to several of them.
>
> Though the therapist did not consider himself to be director of a dating bureau, he was a sensitive clinician. He asked Ralph what kind of a woman he wanted the therapist to fix him up with. Ralph, not expecting the response he got, became stymied. He told the therapist that he had not given much thought to the type of woman he wanted. Upon further reflection, Ralph realized that he was so frightened of seeking out a woman that he could not even reach the point of picturing himself with one.

The case of Ralph suggests that no matter how bizarre a patient's request or how baffling a presenting problem, the sensitive therapist who wants to help the unattached man or woman tries to begin where the client is and help him to articulate, explore, and observe just what and why it is wanted. When the clinician does not impose an agenda on the prospective patient nor quickly redefine the problem, the patient usually feels better understood. If patients are free to talk, they are usually enabled to explore conflicts in more detail and expose idiosyncratic dynamics of which they were not previously aware. When practitioners hear their prospective patients' prescriptions about how they want their problems solved, it is tempting to show them other ways and means. In the initial interviews particularly, this punctures the patient's hopes and fantasies too abruptly. Meeting clients where they are emotionally usually helps them to talk about themselves in more detail.

The Prospective Patient's Situation

To make a full psychosexual assessment of unattached patients, it is important to be aware of the circumstances in which they live. If the prospective patient is living with parents, it will be helpful to know how much the parents are aiding and abetting their offspring's single status. Sometimes those the patient lives with can reinforce latent resistances. Further, when the practitioners are aware of the patient's social context, they can better sensitize themselves to the values, proscriptions, and prescriptions that the patient's ethnic group and other reference groups champion. As an illustration, much pressure is placed on an Orthodox Jewish man or woman to marry, but less so on single men and women in other ethnic groups. As another example, a religious Catholic might feel less inclined to have premarital sex than would a single member of another religious group. The same could be said about role-sets and behaviors prescribed and proscribed by different socioeconomic groups. Role injunctions set by different reference groups are internalized by all individuals; deviating from them can create anxiety (Stein and Cloward 1958).

When patients deviate or would like to deviate from the values their social contexts have prescribed, it is almost inevitable that they will have mixed feelings about it. Sometimes it is difficult for the therapist to recognize the ambivalence because the patient may project one side of the ambivalence onto a parent, religious group, or some important significant other, and it can appear particularly in the initial interviews that the patient is just dealing with an oppositional parent and/or reference group.

> Penelope, age 29, in her second interview with her male therapist, told him she wanted to move out of her parents' home, get her own apartment, and start dating. "However," she informed her therapist, "my parents set up all kinds of roadblocks. They threaten to stop talking to me, resent my relationships with others, and are very antagonistic." When the therapist asked Penelope how she felt about her family's opposition, Penelope began to sob. She realized how much she wanted their approval and really was "torn" within herself as to what she wanted to do.

The Patient's History

As mentioned in Chapter 2, each individual's past shapes his or her present adaptation and functioning. In order to help unattached men or women move toward more closeness with others and not be fearful of intimacy, a great deal of their treatment should consist of the clinician helping them see how they recapitulate their pasts in the present.

Because unattached men and women have a strong tendency to turn potential spouses into parental figures, it is essential for the practitioner to know how these patients have experienced their parents. Furthermore, what is absolutely imperative in understanding the patient's attitudes and behavior is not so much of what actually transpired between the patient and parents, but what meaning the patient gives to those events.

> Oscar, age 42, was in therapy because he was convinced any woman who would get to know him would reject him. As his history unfolded, it became clear that what heavily influenced Oscar's conviction about being rejected was the fact that when he was 3 his sister was born. Oscar's mother then turned a great deal of her attention away from him and toward his sister. This made Oscar believe he was unlovable and rejectable. Instead of allowing himself to feel angry about his mother's movement away from him, Oscar turned his anger against himself and persisted in viewing himself as "a sad sack."

An extremely important dimension of a patient's history, particularly an unattached patient, is how the parents related to each other. If a youngster is reared in an atmosphere where parents love and respect each other and communicate well, the child will tend to replicate this behavior with others, particularly as he or she relates to the opposite sex. Furthermore, most people tend to expect members of the opposite sex to relate to them the way the parent of the opposite sex related to his or her spouse/partner.

Inasmuch as the unattached usually have experienced their parents as having tense relationships, the therapist wants to examine the patient's impressions and memories of the parental relationship in detail. Usually the therapist and patient will find repetitions of the parental interactions in the patient's modus vivendi.

> Nancy, age 31, found that she was in one battle after another with a series of men and that is why she sought therapy. When the therapist examined her history, she learned that Nancy was a witness to many parental arguments throughout her childhood and into her teenage years. In her seventh interview Nancy said with genuine emotion, "I never really believed that men and women could love each other. I really thought they were enemies."

As was suggested in Chapter 2, much of the history gathered by the clinician is the patient's psychosexual history. Not only are the facts important, but how the patient experienced early life is crucial. Does the patient have any impressions or memories of being breast fed? What does the patient think weaning was all about? How was toilet training? What about receiving sexual information? How did the patient feel about his or her siblings? What was school like? These and other facts will go a long way in helping the clinician formulate a comprehensive assessment of the patient's personality and functioning.

In focusing on the contribution of the patient's history and its relationship to current functioning, the practitioner should consider not only the history of the patient's adverse experiences and their meaning, but also, as Helen Perlman (1957) advised:

> The history of his successful or unsuccessful adaptation to them—his "solution" of his difficulties. . . . by retreat, by entrenchment, by blind fighting, or by compromise, detour, and constructive substitutions—this history of his development as a problem-encountering, problem-solving human being may provide . . . an understanding of what the client suffers from and what the extent of his coping ability is likely to be. [p. 176]

The Patient's Psychic Structure

Psychodynamic theory can provide the practitioner with much help in the assessment process, an essential component of all therapy, with its perspective on psychic structure. According to psychodynamic theory, the human psyche is comprised of id, ego, and superego (Freud 1939). The id, the most primitive part of the mind, is the repository of the drives and is concerned with their gratification. The ego is the executive part of the personality and mediates between the inner world of id drives (sex and aggression) and superego commands, and the demands of the external world. Some of the ego functions are judgment, reality testing, frustration tolerance, impulse control, and interpersonal relations (sometimes called "object relations."). The ego also forms defenses against anxiety. Some of the defenses are projection—ascribing to others what cannot be tolerated within the self, denial, repression, and reaction formation—saying and doing the opposite of what part of the self feels, for example, I love, I do not hate.

By assessing a patient's ego strengths and weaknesses, the therapist can better determine how the patient is adapting. The more severe the patient's disturbances, the less operative are the ego functions and vice versa. Knowing how the patient's ego copes with frustration, impulse control, interpersonal relations, and so forth, helps the therapist set realistic treatment goals, arrive at a prognosis, and plan interventions. If, for example, the patient's ego is such that it cannot observe its functions too well, that is, "the observing ego" is weak, providing the patient with insight is usually contraindicated. Or, if the patient's object relations are weak, this would probably indicate that an intensive working relationship with the therapist, that is, a strong therapeutic alliance, is not tenable.

The superego is the judge or censor of the mind and is essentially the product of interpersonal experiences. It is divided into two parts: the conscience and the ego ideal. The conscience is that part of the superego which forbids and admonishes; the ego ideal is the storehouse of ethical imperatives, values, and morals. A patient with a punitive and exacting superego usually has strong id wishes (sex and aggression) which are intolerable to him or her and cause much pain and anxiety. Many unattached men and women, rather than constantly live with unbearable pain and anxiety, arrange for the superego to admonish them and to deny themselves pleasure. These inhibited, constricted patients are individuals who defend themselves from facing their strong id wishes by forming strong defenses of denial, repression, and reaction formation. In order eventually to relate intimately, these patients need to diminish the severity of their superegos by having a positive experience with an accepting therapist who will be experienced as a benign superego.

> Martin, age 36, was a guilt-ridden man who felt "ugly, stupid, inept, and a poor sexual partner." In investigating Martin's self-loathing and intense masochism, the therapist learned that Martin hated himself for his chronic masturbation and murderous fantasies. When Martin clearly saw that the therapist did not punish him or judge him, but sought to understand him, that is, become a benign superego, Martin's self-esteem and self-confidence improved considerably. When he did not have to erect a punitive superego to castigate himself, Martin could like himself much more.

In assessing the unattached individual's functioning, it is important to observe how the patient's id, ego, and superego interact. For example, a promiscuous man or woman who does not sustain relationships may have a punitive superego that does not allow for closeness and intimacy. Therefore, this individual can only permit id gratification as long as it is intermittent and brief. The patient may repress thoughts of intimacy and deny dependency longings.

Very often when unattached men and women cannot tolerate their infantile wishes of dependency and desires to regress, they project these forbidden wishes onto prospective partners, thus defending themselves from anxiety.

> Lucy, a woman of 34, came to treatment because she could not seem to find men whom she could respect. She found herself demeaning them, controlling them, and withdrawing from them. As therapy moved on, it became clear that Lucy did not like herself as a woman, viewing herself as a "second-class citizen." By projecting her self-image onto men and devaluing them, Lucy could avoid facing her own weak self-image and save herself from some suffering.

The psychic structure may be compared to a car (Strean 1994). The id could be viewed as an engine; the ego as the driver, and the superego as the backseat driver. An assessment of the patient's psychic structure—id, ego, and superego—and the way they interact can help the therapist better understand what hinders the patient from enjoying an intimate relationship.

The Assessment

When the patient's presenting problems have been clarified and he or she has been helped to feel comfortable in the initial interviews, and after gathering the pertinent data, the therapist is ready to formulate a psychosexual assessment. We should remind ourselves, however, that the gathering of data is never a static process; new information on the patient's current problems, history, and cultural background is always forthcoming. The assessment, therefore, is always being enlarged and modified.

The process of assessment is an attempt to ascertain what troubles the patient, why it is troubling, and how it seems to contribute to the problems of being unattached. Such professional judgments should be checked and rechecked to assure their validity and reliability (Siporin 1975). The assessment takes into consideration how the patient's history is being recapitulated in his current interpersonal relationships; how his psychic structure (id, ego and superego) is utilized to create and sustain interpersonal and internal conflicts; what his modes of relating to the therapist reveal about the way he copes with intimate relationships, and how his social environment aids and abets his conflicts.

In the assessment phase of psychotherapy, the practitioner seeks to explain the patient's problems with intimacy and why she remains unattached. Is Ms. Smith's inability to enjoy sexual pleasure a function of her oedipal conflicts where she turns men into forbidden father figures stolen from mother? Or, does she make men into male siblings whom she envies? Or, does Ms. Smith turn men into the engulfing mother of her past? Or, is her inability to form intimate relationships with men a combination of all these factors and are other variables operative as well? How strong or weak are Ms. Smith's ego functions as she tries to cope with her struggles? Is her superego punitive? What wishes and fantasies of hers does she punish herself for? How much of her maladaptive behavior is a regression or a fixation? What is the contribution of her social environment and current role network? What fantasies does she harbor when she falls in love? Or, has she ever fallen in love? These and other questions should be answered by the practitioner when attempting to make an assessment of Ms. Smith. If the assessment is comprehensive, valid, and reliable, then an appropriate therapeutic modality can be selected and an individualized treatment process can be effected.

Choosing the Therapeutic Modality

In most instances, but far from all, the psychodynamically oriented therapist favors individual long-term therapy for the treatment of the unattached man or woman. There are several reasons for this bias. First, inasmuch as unattached men and women have problems in either forming, sustaining, or enjoying long-term relationships, it would seem logical that when they have to deal with a long-term relationship with their therapists, their anxieties, defenses, habitual defenses, and usual ways of relating will become issues in the therapeutic relationship. As they examine their transference reactions to the therapist, they will be able to note the similarity of their transference responses to their characteristic ways of relating to others. Second, many of the difficulties of unattached men and women are unconscious; they have little awareness of what wishes, defenses, history, fantasies, and superego mandates are at work. An orientation to therapy that focuses on an examination of unconscious matters seems to hold much promise. Third, the problems of unattached men and women are rarely superficial. These men and women usually have tried many avenues of help before coming to a therapist. Consequently, they need plenty of time to uncover their deep conflicts. Finally, as Meissner (1978) has pointed out, long-term individual therapy requires the patient to assume a large part of the responsibility for his or her personal growth and change. When men and women learn to face their own intrapsychic and interpersonal problems with their therapists, they usually become better partners in intimate relationships.

Although long-term individual treatment does appear to be the treatment of choice for many unattached men and women, from time to time some individuals who are already involved in a relationship want to be seen in treatment as a couple. Some of those patients who would like to participate in conjoint treatment are already in individual therapy but wish to focus on their interaction with their mates.

When a patient already in individual therapy wants to modify the treatment plan and be seen in conjoint therapy, it is always a good idea for all concerned to evaluate the individual therapy to which the patient is already committed. Occasionally, there are unresolved transference and/or countertransference problems or unresolved resistance and/or counterresistance problems in the individual treatment that are being acted out as conjoint therapy is being planned. Yet, conjoint treatment does have some unique features that can help certain couples mature.

Conjoint treatment attempts to treat the neurotic interaction between two individuals rather than treat the individuals themselves. Advocates of this approach point out that dysfunctional relationships often are the product of incompatible role expectations and a lack of role complementarity, which conjoint treatment can address (Ackerman 1958). Also, according to Martin (1976), the therapist in conjoint therapy is better able to limit destructive behavior and facilitate the development of the observing ego of each partner, enabling them to test reality more effectively.

Some of the disadvantages of conjoint therapy are that most of the time the unconscious motives of the individuals cannot appear spontaneously, and that confidentiality is not assured. Thus, many individual secrets are not forthcoming. Because of the nature of the format, the dyad can use it to discharge complaints without getting to the individual wishes and defenses which keep these complaints alive. With its emphasis on the present, conjoint therapy can ignore important dimensions of the individual's history which may be important variables contributing toward the couple's conflicts.

Advocates of conjoint therapy tend to overlook the fact that to participate in this therapy requires reasonably strong ego functions in both partners. The man and woman, for conjoint therapy to succeed, have to be able to identify with one another, empathize with each other, tolerate frustration and anxiety, modulate hostility, and share the therapist. Many individuals are not capable of doing the work that conjoint therapy necessitates because certain functions are not sufficiently developed.

Conjoint therapy seems to be the treatment of choice for those dyads who have many ego functions intact. These are individuals who communicate well with each other, can share the therapist without experiencing too much sibling rivalry and have many conflict-free areas in their individual and interpersonal functioning. In effect, mature, well-integrated individuals seem to be the best candidates for conjoint therapy.

There are some unattached men and women who are in intensely symbiotic relationships. These are couples who usually have many interpersonal problems but cannot separate from each other and be autonomous. They seek conjoint therapy because it is a treatment that does not separate them. With these couples, the therapist must begin where they are and see them together. When they are stronger as individuals, they can eventually become candidates for individual therapy.

Both conjoint therapy and individual therapy may be long or short. However, there are many individuals who strongly fear a sustained long-term treatment approach. They have profound fears of closeness, exposure, and commitment; usually they are very suspicious and even paranoid. Often, when paranoid individuals who fear intimacy are offered short-term therapy, they feel much less threatened. They may move on to more extensive treatment when they feel less anxious. However, even if patients cannot move on, short-term work is usually better than no treatment at all.

Those unattached men and women who cannot tolerate either individual or conjoint therapy may feel more secure in a group. There they can hide if they have to, and can feel less humiliated when they see that other people have problems similar to theirs. Among the disadvantages of groups for the unattached is the fostering of mutual communication of hopelessness, or the potential for member who are very destructive to disrupt group inter-action and cohesion (Grunebaum et al. 1969).

The Treatment Process

Regardless of whether treatment is long or short, indi-vidual, dyadic, or group, certain phenomena such as transference, countertransference, resistance, and coun-terresistance always manifest themselves. Furthermore, certain treatment procedures such as clarification, confrontation, and interpretation are almost always part of every therapist's role repertoire. I would like to review these important parts of the treatment process and show their applicability to the treatment of the unattached patient.

Transference

Because of our unique histories, ego functioning, superego mandates, values, and social circumstances, each of us brings to every relationship wishes, fears, anxieties, hopes, pressures, defenses, and many more subjective non-rational factors. These variables that influence our current role interactions have evolved from previous relationships and may not always be appropriate in the situation in which they are being expressed. Inasmuch as these universal phenomena are largely unconscious, we cannot easily prevent their occurrence. Furthermore, they emerge in all of our relationships: marriage, the classroom, business, friendships, and, of course, therapy (Freud, 1926).

The intimate relationship of patient and therapist recapitulates the feelings and fantasies as well as the emotionally charged experiences that the patient had with parents, siblings, and others. If clinicians do not understand and relate to how they are experienced by their patients, they cannot be too helpful. All patients respond to their therapists' interventions in terms of transference. If the patient loves the therapist, he or she will in all probability warmly endorse the therapist's comments, no matter how valid or invalid. By the same token, if the therapist reminds the patient of a hated parent or sibling, no matter how timely and accurate the therapist's comments, they will probably be rejected. Finally, if the patient is ambivalent toward the therapist, he or she will respond ambivalently to most therapeutic interventions.

Much of psychodynamically oriented therapy is an attempt to help patients understand why they respond to the therapist the way they do. Assisting the patient in feeling and comprehending transference reactions is one of the major means of helping the patient overcome the inhibitions she has in becoming intimately attached to a mate.

Because the unattached patient is usually rejecting, albeit unconsciously, prospective mates, he will inevitably want to reject the therapist. Sometimes the rejection is subtle; on other occasions, it is direct. In either case, the competent and empathetic clinician tries to separate his or her own reactions to the patient's transference responses and, instead, attempts to help the patient get in touch with from where and whence they come.

> Ken, a man in his early fifties, had been divorced three times. He referred to all of his ex-wives as "cold, hostile bitches who did not give a damn." In his therapy with a woman who was about his own age, at first he was polite and deferential. However, after about three months of weekly therapy, Ken began to come late for appointments, was silent for long periods of time, and seemed to be moderately depressed.

When Ken's therapist wondered if perhaps she was not helping him sufficiently because he seemed less enthusiastic about their work, he responded with one and two word answers. However, when the therapist said, "Maybe you wonder if I give a damn," Ken sat forward and seemed startled. He then blurted out, "Of course you don't give a damn. You are here to make a living. If you met me elsewhere, you wouldn't have a thing to do with me."

On the therapist's saying, "Then I, too, must be a cold, hostile bitch," Ken was able to feel very understood. He talked about having "a bitch of a mother" and was "always ready" to experience every woman that way.

If clinicians genuinely appreciate the fact that transference is always present in the treatment, they can evaluate their therapeutic results more objectively. If patients hate their therapists, they will not move in the therapy because they have to spite their helpers. If they love their therapists, they will want to cooperate and show they have been helped. Sometimes, however, patients idealize their therapists to ward off hostility.

Janet, a woman of 35, was in treatment because she was "always being rejected by men." In her therapy with a male practitioner, she was consistently heaping praise on him and telling him what a gifted clinician he was. When the therapist realized that Janet was doing very little in her therapy other than being ingratiating, he began to wonder if "the lady doth protest too much."

On being told by the therapist that she was full of compliments in every session (which was twice a week), Janet became pale and then sobbed for about ten minutes. When she composed herself, she said with much conviction and insight, "I've always felt that the only way to get along with men is to lick their asses. They are all pompous and egocentric and you are, too! My father was that way and I hated his guts."

A transference reaction that is quite common among unattached patients is making the therapist "a dirty old man" (or woman), projecting their unacceptable id wishes onto the practitioner.

Ian, a man in his mid-20s who was being treated for impotence, acknowledged that he felt intimidated by his female therapist. When the therapist explored with Ian just what it was about her behavior that intimidated him, Ian responded, "I feel that you use your soft, sexy voice to try to trap me. When you see that I can get excited, you'll move away from me. I know this for sure."

As Ian's therapy progressed, it became evident that he was very attracted to his therapist, but found it difficult to acknowledge this to himself. Instead, he made the therapist an active seducer out to trap him. Therapist and patient later learned that Ian had experienced his mother as "a seducer who then castrated," and he tended unconsciously to turn most women into this figure.

Although transference reactions are almost always traceable to childhood, there is not always a simple correspondence between past and present. In spite of an occasional direct repetition—such as when the patient is convinced that the therapist is an exact replica of a mother, father, spouse, or sibling (as was true in the case of Ian)—there is frequently a "compensatory fantasy" (Fine 1982) to make up for what was lacking in childhood; that is, patients fantasize that the therapist is somebody they would have liked as a parent or sibling.

As suggested earlier in this chapter, it can often be inferred from fantasies and dreams that overt positive and loving feelings expressed toward the practitioner may be covering up negative and hateful feelings. Similarly, hostile statements toward the therapist can defend against warm feelings.

It is important to emphasize that no patient is exempt from transference reactions. Transference exists in all relationships. In therapy, transference reactions can be used profitably to help the patient see how he or she distorts relationships and then suffers the consequences. This is particularly true for unattached patients who have a strong tendency to turn others into hateful individuals from their pasts. It should also be emphasized that in helping patients understand their transference reactions, the therapist has to proceed cautiously. One cannot immediately call to patients' attention their transference reactions whenever they occur. Patients must be able to experience them over and over again before they are able to acknowledge them, see how they create them, and why they need them.

Countertransference

Transference reactions of the therapist toward the patient are called *countertransference*. It refers to those wishes, fantasies, anxieties, defenses, and superego mandates of the therapist that color her perceptions of the patient and influences her choice of therapeutic modality, treatment interventions, and everything else done or not done in the treatment situation. Therapists can make patients their parents, siblings, or other important figures from their past. Often they, too, have "compensatory countertransference fantasies" and turn their patients into lovers, friends, or colleagues (Strean 1993a, b).

As Abend (1989) stated in his paper "Countertransference and Psychoanalytic Technique," "Freud's original idea that countertransference means unconscious interference with [the therapist's] ability to understand patients has been broadened during the past forty years: current usage often includes all of the emotional reactions at work" (p. 374). This view has received much support in the clinical literature. Slakter (1987) referred to countertransference as "all those reactions of [the therapist] to the patient that may help or hinder treatment" (p. 3). Rather than viewing countertransference as a periodic unconscious interference, there is now a rather large psychotherapeutic literature on countertransference with most authors acknowledging that it is as everpresent as transference and must be constantly studied by all therapists, from the neophyte to the very experienced (Abend 1982, 1989, Brenner 1985, Fine 1982, Strean 1991).

In working with unattached patients, there are a few common countertransference responses. One of them is a tendency to parentify the patient. Feeling compassionate toward the patient because he or she appears lonely and vulnerable, it is tempting for the therapist to want to take

over the patient's life. However, when patients are controlled and dominated, they begin to feel hostile toward
the practitioner, fear their autonomy is being relin-
quished, and may leave treatment prematurely.

> Holly, a 31-year-old woman, was in treatment because she
> didn't "know how to get along with men." She frequently
> found herself rejected by men after a few dates and did not
> know why.
>
> Helpless, very dependent, and often feeling hopeless,
> Holly frequently tried to get her male therapist to advise
> her how to get dates, how to converse with them, and how
> to keep them. Her therapist, feeling very sorry for Holly
> because of her lack of success with men, gave Holly the
> advice she wanted.
>
> Inasmuch as the therapist unwittingly fostered Holly's
> dependency by repeatedly advising her, her self-
> confidence and self-esteem did not develop. Rather, Holly
> felt more like a helpless infant. She eventually gave up on
> her therapy, feeling "hopeless, helpless, anguished, and
> angry."

Another countertransference reaction that the unattached patient can induce is one in which the therapist
becomes a substitute boyfriend or girlfriend and unconsciously tries to become a better partner than anyone the
patient has met or could meet.

> George, a 42-year-old man, was in treatment because he
> found himself feeling uncomfortable with women who fell
> in love with him. In his treatment sessions with his female
> therapist, George was full of criticism toward the women

he dated. Rather than subject his criticism to examination, his therapist tended to agree with it. All this was temporarily reassuring for George. However, when this therapist went on vacation, George left treatment. He told another therapist, a male, whom he saw subsequently, that his first therapist "was out to make me and that was too much."

Many unattached men and women tend to present themselves as victims and find it difficult to take responsibility for their own contributions to their sad plights. It is tempting for the therapist to confront these patients with their own provocative behavior, because the patients who appear arrogant and grandiose toward the world do induce irritation in the therapist. When therapeutic interventions are sparked by hostile feelings toward the patient, they rarely are effective.

Florence, age 42, had been divorced three times. In her therapy with a male, she projected a great deal of the marital difficulties onto the men. Although her therapist was correct in his assessment when he told Florence that she found it difficult to see her own role in the marriages, he was feeling very irritated with her and that came across. Florence reacted to his affect and became even more vituperative in her sessions. It was only after the therapist could acknowledge his anger toward Florence and realize that he was experiencing his patient as if she were his older contemptuous sister from the past that the therapy could progress.

Therapists are human and therefore can feel hostility toward some of their patients some of the time. They may feel a little anger toward one or two much of the time. Just as a negative transference has to be understood, a therapist's negative countertransference has to be understood. Frequently when the practitioner does not like a client, it is because the latter reminds him of a disliked parent or sibling. Often a negative countertransference is activated because the patient demonstrates attitudes and behavior that the therapist cannot tolerate in himself.

> Eric, in his early thirties, was in treatment with a male therapist. Eric sought help because he found himself physically beating his girlfriends from time to time and was worried about getting in trouble with the law if he continued. When his therapist found himself hating Eric and wanting to slug him when he heard about his abusive behavior, he had to spend a lot of time and energy resolving his hatred.
>
> What the therapist discovered from examining himself was that he, too, harbored much resentment toward some women in his life. Although he had not hit any women, he had fantasies of doing so. In effect, Eric was doing what the therapist would have liked to do, but could not tolerate in himself. He wanted to punish Eric for doing what he, the therapist, wanted to do.

Countertransference, like transference, appears in all therapeutic modalities. In conjoint therapy the therapist can join with one partner and be against the other, indulge both of them, or hate both of them. Just as there is no such thing as a patient who has "no transference," there is no such thing as a therapist who had "no countertransference."

When clinicians allow themselves to be similar to their patients and realize they are always having subjective feelings toward their therapy partners, they foster a safer and more intimate therapeutic climate. From a constant study of their countertransference reactions, they not only learn a lot about themselves, but also learn a great deal about what their patients want to induce in them.

> Dale, a young woman in her late twenties, was in therapy with a man a few years older than she. The therapist discovered from the beginning that in every session with Dale he was having strong, erotic fantasies toward her. Although he examined his own wishes and anxieties, the fantasies about Dale continued unabated. After a few discussions with a colleague, the therapist became aware of the fact that Dale was actively trying to seduce him. Further, the therapist realized that this was Dale's way of trying to weaken him as a therapist and defeat the therapy. When the therapist could emotionally experience Dale's wish to defeat him, he did not feel as flattered by her seductive behavior. Then the therapy could progress.

A practitioner who is able to consistently confront countertransference reactions without being too influenced by irrational love, hate, and ambivalence is in an excellent position to help patients resolve their problems. Working with unattached men and women requires the clinician to deal constantly with intense countertransference reactions. That is one of the reasons why therapeutic work with them is endlessly challenging.

Resistance and Counterresistance

Anybody who has attempted to help another human being in psychotherapy has consistently observed a universal paradox. Although all patients want to lessen their pain and enjoy more pleasure, they also have a strong desire to maintain the status quo and not alter their modus vivendi. Regardless of the setting in which they are seen and regardless of the modality in which they are treated, all patients present obstacles to their feeling better and functioning better (Strean 1990). Therapists who accept resistance as a fact of therapeutic life will not be surprised when they hear a divorced spouse say repeatedly, "Love cannot exist for very long." They will not be shocked when they hear the celibate man or woman aver, "Sex is not for reasonable people." And, they won't be particularly angry when they hear many unattached men and women state, "Psychotherapy is a waste of time."

Although most patients welcome the idea of pouring their hearts out to a quiet, attentive, empathetic listener, sooner or later the therapy become painful and creates anxiety. As patients discover parts of themselves that have been repressed, such as sexual and aggressive fantasies, they may become silent and evasive, come late for sessions, question the value of therapy, berate the therapist for his or her lack of competence, or want to quit therapy altogether.

When patients stop talking about themselves and cease examining themselves, this is called resistance. Resistance is any action or attitude that impedes the course of therapeutic work. Inasmuch as every patient, to some extent, wants to preserve the status quo, all therapy must be carried on in the face of some resistance.

At the beginning of this chapter, I discussed some of the initial resistances that all unattached patients manifest. What is important to stress is that resistance is par for the whole course of treatment. Patients continue to defend themselves against anxiety by denying their problems, repressing their feelings, rationalizing their provocations, and projecting their uncertainties onto the therapist and others. They continue to derive pleasure from some of their infantile pursuits and do not immediately stop punishing themselves for their real and/or imagined sins (Strean 1990).

What is important for the therapist of the unattached patient to recognize is that the presence of a resistance always means that the patient feels in danger and is trying to ward off impending pain. All clinicians should recognize that resistance is something not good or bad; it is an unconscious operation that the patient uses to protect himself or herself.

Resistance is not created by therapy. The therapeutic situation activates similar types of anxiety that are aroused in the patient's life and the patient then uses habitual mechanisms to oppose the therapy and the therapist (Greenson, 1967).

One of the main values in studying resistances is that therapist and patient can become clearer about what is inhibiting the patient from moving into closer, more intimate relationships.

When Calvin, age 43, habitually came late for his interviews, his female therapist wondered out loud what was
difficult about coming to the sessions. Calvin told his
therapist that he was bored by their interviews and dis-
couraged with the treatment. When the therapist asked
what she was doing to make the sessions boring, Calvin
reported that sooner or later he found all women boring
and unstimulating. Later in his therapy, Calvin learned
that underneath his boredom was a fear of his strong
dependency wishes. To ward off the danger of becoming
dependent on his therapist, Calvin unconsciously pushed
her away.

Resistances take many forms and often manifest themselves subtly. The client can become overcompliant, so-
maticize conflicts, or become unduly deferential with the
therapist.

Beulah, a divorced woman in her forties, was extremely
deferential and cooperative with her female therapist.
When the therapist began to feel manipulated by Beulah's
oversolicitousness and felt a bit uncomfortable in the
interviews, she shared her impression with Beulah that
she always appeared like "a good girl." Exploration of
Beulah's resistance revealed that she felt quite competitive
with her therapist but feared she would be in danger if she
revealed her "negative" feelings.

What is sometimes overlooked in a discussion of resistances is that the same resistive behavior may have
different meanings for different patients. Although lateness for Calvin, in an earlier example, was his way of

showing his fear of intimacy, lateness for another individual or dyad may express a fear of showing aggression, or an anxiety about sexual fantasies, or some other danger. The meaning of a patient's resistance is unique to the patient and it may take many sessions for that meaning to be determined.

Just as the term *countertransference* refers to the therapist's transference reactions toward the patient, the term *counterresistance* refers to the therapist's resistances in the treatment situation. Therapists, like patients, can be late for interviews, absent themselves from sessions, be delinquent in asking for fees, charge too much or too little for service, and so on. Very often a patient's resistance can be reinforced by a therapist's counterresistance.

> Arthur, a widower of 62, spent a great deal of his time in therapy discussing politics, social problems, the theatre, and other issues far away from himself. His female therapist found herself joining in the discussions. Although the chats were pleasant, Arthur remained a lonely man without any social contacts.
>
> When the therapist recognized how she was colluding with Arthur in resisting the therapy, she began to study the treatment situation more carefully. She realized that it frightened her to hear about Arthur's strong passivity, clinging dependency, and intense anger. Later it became apparent that Arthur was afraid of facing these same issues. Patient and therapist were busy protecting each other and themselves.

From the moment the patient calls for a consultation until the termination of the contact, the therapist has fantasies and feelings that can always influence the client's behavior in the treatment. Often therapists should take some responsibility when patients absent themselves from sessions, are late, do not pay fees, or show some other forms of resistance (Langs 1981, Strean 1990, 1993a).

Interventive Procedures

I have been stressing that one of the best things a therapist can be is a good listener. As patients pour out their hearts, they feel valued by a quiet, empathetic listener, and their self-esteem usually rises. Then they are able to examine transference reactions, resistances, the impact of their histories on their current adaptation, as well as other important issues.

Therapists, however, have to be more than listeners. At times they must confront patients with behavior and attitudes that are aiding and abetting their unattached states. As we have seen from some of the case vignettes in this chapter, it is important for the therapist to help the patient examine issues such as lateness to sessions, absences, non-payment of fees, oversolicitousness, and deferential behavior.

Very often when patients are confronted with their transference reactions and other resistive behavior, they become defensive because they feel attacked. Providing the therapist is not acting in a belligerent fashion, many unattached patients often need help in determining why they are so ready to experience an exploration of some of the maladaptive behavior as a punishment or attack.

The decisive question with regard to the therapist's statement is not whether it is correct but how the patient reacts to it, and in turn what the therapist does with the patient's reactions (Fine 1968). Perhaps in the majority of cases the therapist offers the "correct" confrontative statement or interpretation; however, if the patient needs to oppose the therapist, that is what the therapist must attend to. As I suggested earlier in this chapter, every response to a therapist's statements or queries is guided by the patient's current transference position. If the patient feels like a guilty child, then everything the therapist says will be viewed as an attacking punishment. If the patient feels like a lover or potential lover, every utterance of the therapist will sound like a potential seduction.

Confrontation leads to the next therapeutic procedure, clarification. Clarification refers to those activities of the therapist that aim at placing the patient's behavior in sharp focus and examining the issues that motivate it (Greenson 1967). For example, after a patient is confronted with habitual tardiness to sessions, what might become clarified are the patient's hidden resentments about therapy and the therapist.

The next step after clarification is interpretation. To interpret is to make an unconscious phenomenon, such as a defense or a wish, conscious. In effect, it means to make conscious the unconscious meaning of a specific psychological event. As an illustration of an interpretation, the therapist may say, "You are late to our sessions because you experience me as the authoritarian father of your past. You find it difficult to discuss your resentments toward me openly because you are worried I will retaliate as your father did. Coming late is your way of telling me you find it hard to be with me."

After an issue such as lateness is confronted, clarified, and interpreted, the next step is working through. Working through refers to the repetitive, progressive explorations of the patient's attitudes and behavior that eventually lead to insight and behavioral changes.

Although the aforementioned treatment procedures are crucial in the therapy of a patient, what is equally crucial is that the patient is listened to carefully and attentively and feels genuinely accepted by the therapist. Brilliant interpretations of therapists who are ambivalent or hostile toward the patient have little impact, but occasional lapses of a loving, caring therapist are usually overlooked by the patient.

4

The Case of
Grace Johnson

It was a brisk, sunny day in October and as I was walking to my office, I noticed how beautiful the scenery was in Central Park. It was a day that made one feel exhilarated — it was good to be alive!

As if she fitted in with the bright day, when she saw me enter the waiting room, Grace Johnson had a broad smile. Her blonde hair, gorgeous figure, and well-tailored clothes made me feel that I was about to meet an outstanding actress. She looked about 30 years old, and was 5 feet 8 inches tall. Her smile broadened more as I moved toward her, and in an exuberant voice she said, "Hi, I'm Grace Johnson. It's great to meet you!" I could hear the enthusiasm in my own voice as I introduced myself. As I led the way to my consultation room, I said to myself, "I bet she has no difficulty meeting men. She seems so smooth."

After Grace and I were seated, there was a momentary silence. I usually wait for the patient to begin the session, feeling that it is helpful to see what comes out spontaneously. If the patient doesn't say anything, after about ten seconds I'll initiate the dialogue because I do not want too much anxiety to mount in the patient, nor do I think it is desirable for the patient to feel self-conscious at the very beginning of the first session. When ten seconds of silence elapse, I routinely ask something like, "What brings you in?" I did not have to do this with Grace. She was prepared to talk about herself and her problems.

"This is not my first round of therapy," Grace began. "I have to tell you that you are my fourth shrin . . ., I mean, my fourth therapist." When I noted that she was embarrassed about calling me a shrink, I tried to help her feel safer by saying, "As you know, most people refer to people like me as shrinks." Grace laughed and showed some relief. Then she suggested, "I guess you'd be interested in hearing about my experiences in the therapeutic arena." I told her I was interested.

Although Grace was charming, friendly, and an attractive woman, after I was with her for no more than five minutes, I began to hypothesize silently that she had been in some kind of fight with her previous therapist and wondered when this was going to occur with me. She had referred to her therapeutic experiences as "rounds"— integral parts of a boxing match. They took place in an "arena," a place where gladiators met. Also, maybe she had some concern about reducing me in size inasmuch as she was uncomfortable about "shrinking" me.

Grace informed me that she had had two male therapists but her last one was a woman. When I asked, "What happened with her?" Grace smiled coyly and said, "I rejected the two men and the woman rejected me."

With regard to her experiences with the two male therapists, Grace told me that initially she felt well understood and liked them. However, after about six months she felt very bored. The first therapist, according to Grace, spoke repetitively about her disappointment with her father, so much so that she could usually anticipate what he was going to say. The second therapist said nothing informative or insightful and so he, too, became boring.

In her therapy with the woman therapist, Grace reported that she was told she was insufficiently trusting and had a great deal of unexpressed hostility. Grace never did consider whether or not these observations were valid. Instead, she felt very hurt by what she experienced as hostile criticism and left treatment. As Grace reviewed some of her interactions with her female therapist, she made a reference or two to her mother. I then asked her about her mother and was told she was a social worker in private practice, a successful family therapist. Grace further described her mother as "very attractive," "very bright," and with a "short fuse." Mother was very contemptuous of father and demeaned him in front of Grace and her younger siblings, a sister two years younger, and a brother three years younger "who was mother's favorite." Grace went on to talk about her mother with tears and some anger. "She often hit me, frequently did not talk to me, and always seemed to be finding fault with me."

Grace described her father as "a nice man but very quiet." He appeared to be very intimidated by his wife and coped by withdrawing. Grace always wished she could have depended on her father to influence her mother to be kinder to her; however, this never happened.

Grace's relationships with both of her siblings was "very competitive." She did not feel particularly close to either of them and at the initial consultation with me was having very little to do with them, even though they both lived in New York City.

Grace had many close friends during her childhood and adolescence. She was a good student throughout high school and college. In high school she was a cheerleader and graduated as valedictorian. In college Grace also did well. She received a master's degree in education and for seven years enjoyed her work as an elementary school teacher.

At this point in the initial interview, as I was reflecting on Grace's many ego strengths—she was a good student, an excellent teacher, quite popular, and seemed congenial—I reminded myself of her latent aggression, which had manifested itself early in the interview. Perhaps it was more than a coincidence that Grace then announced her main reason for seeking therapy at this time. "What I really want from you is help in getting along with men. Every time I'm involved with a guy, sooner or later we have a falling out." Although Grace enjoyed herself emotionally and sexually with the men, sooner or later she got "turned off." Grace had not really learned much in her previous therapy about what was going on inside that prompted her withdrawal from men.

She wanted to begin her therapy on a weekly basis and agreed to pay my usual fee. She told me that she had found the interview "pleasant" and looked forward to seeing me again the following week.

I had a warm and positive feeling toward Grace throughout the session and felt pleased to be working with her. I cautioned myself not to be too enthusiastic or I might overlook her hostility toward men, which of course would include negative reactions toward me. I reminded myself that Grace did not do too well with her previous male therapists and broke up with them quickly and in much the same way she did with her boyfriends. I wondered if some of her animosity toward her father was being acted out with her male friends and therapists. I also hypothesized that she might have identified with her mother's contempt toward her father. Perhaps, too, some of her hostility toward men was related to her unresolved resentment toward her brother.

After the first session, the more I thought about Grace, the more I realized she was full of hurt and anger toward everyone in her family. She experienced her mother as far from nurturing and loving. Her father appeared emotionally unavailable and withdrawn, and she maintained a distance from both siblings. It seemed quite clear that she had not enjoyed a close relationship with any family member. Given her emotional detachment from her parents and siblings, it was reasonably clear that she would have difficulty forming a permanent attachment to a man.

The Initial Interviews

Grace spent her first six sessions talking about a young man, Gordon, whom she had recently met. She described him as "a warm, bright person" who seemed to be "a lot of fun." Similar to how she described the initial interaction with her previous boyfriends, communication and sex with Gordon were very enjoyable.

Grace had a lot to say in the early interviews. I kept my remarks to a minimum. As I have already suggested, quiet listening helps most patients feel valued and usually their self-esteem rises. Also, as patients are given an opportunity to free associate without interruption, they begin to recall events, entertain fantasies, and experience transference reactions. This "dynamic inactivity" of the therapist (Fine 1982) invariably induces a great deal of introspection. This is what happened with Grace. As she continued to explore her relationship with Gordon, Grace began to worry that she would tire of him as she had with the others. I suggested to her that inasmuch as she had experienced a sense of boredom with several men, including her male therapists, perhaps we could try to understand better what activated the boredom.

In response to my suggestion, Grace had a lot to say.

The issue that emerged first was that in every relationship with a man, after a short period Grace felt "gypped" and wanted more from the man. Either the man wasn't bright enough, sexy enough, or considerate enough. As a matter of fact, one of the things that was occupying Grace's current thought was that Gordon, who was a teacher, would not make enough money to support her adequately.

As Grace talked about feeling deprived by the men she dated, I thought of her male therapists who, from her point of view, didn't give her enough. When I mentioned this to Grace, she said with conviction, "No man has ever given me what I wanted or needed. I think the same could be said about my father and my brother David. They never came through for me." In a moving manner, Grace tearfully talked about how she had always yearned for her father to praise her, hug her, and to get her mother to be kind to her; as Grace saw it, "He didn't have it in him." By the end of her third month in therapy, it was not difficult for Grace to see that she was reliving her relationship with her father with her boyfriends. She wanted them to be attentive, generous, and loving fathers to the part of her that felt like their daughter. Instead they, with needs of their own, were treating her as an equal adult.

Sharing her feelings of deprivation, and facing the neglected daughter in herself was very helpful to Grace. For the first time in her adult life she could get in touch emotionally with "the little girl" in herself and see how that little girl influenced her adult behavior, particularly with men. Sensing that I was feeling empathetic toward her and accepting of her feelings, Grace was more able to accept herself.

The Honeymoon Phase

As Grace began her fourth month of treatment, she was feeling "up." She continued to enjoy her relationship with Gordon, was more confident at work, more relaxed with her friends, saw and appreciated her father more, and felt less combative with her mother and siblings. She felt her therapy was helpful, so she increased her sessions to twice a week.

In response to my dynamic inactivity, Grace, in effect, began to experience me as the caring father she always craved. Feeling that she had a loving father on her side, everybody and everything around her appeared loving and lovable. In the first dream that she reported at the end of the fourth month of treatment, she was in a night club on 96th Street in New York City (the location of my office) and an older, gray-haired man asked her to dance. When Grace agreed to dance, the man was a bit clumsy, "dancing a two-step without much grace."

Grace had no difficulty acknowledging that the dream expressed a wish to dance with me, an older father figure. She could even recognize a hidden sexual desire inasmuch as dancing would bring our bodies close together. Grace had some difficulty in facing her wish to knock me down, having made me into a "clumsy" dancer. Although she recognized that "the two step" might have alluded to the twice-a-week therapy, she did not accept my interpretation that my dancing "without grace" might have referred to her, Grace, getting rid of me after some contact (as had happened repeatedly with other men).

Although Grace resisted facing the negative component of the current transference, her life continued to improve. She started to see her father on a regular basis, realized for the first time "what a handsome and kind man" he was, and could even acknowledge some sexual fantasies toward him. Grace realized that she held back her love toward her father because she was always frightened her mother would resent her for it. In her sixth month of treatment, Grace had a dream in which she was about to take a shower with her father and her mother angrily stopped her.

As Grace discussed her libidinal wishes toward her father and simultaneously had thoughts and fantasies involving her mother, her oedipal conflict became more apparent. Just as she was not able to allow herself to get too close to her father because of her mother's possible rebuke, she could only allow herself limited pleasure with men. Her mother's resentment had become part of an internalized punitive superego. Beginning to face her oedipal conflict in more depth and breadth, her transference toward me shifted dramatically.

The First Treatment Crisis

Toward the end of Grace's first year of treatment, I told her I would be taking a vacation of about five weeks. Although I informed her about my vacation a month in advance, Grace was very angry about getting such "short notice." She told me that she felt furious about having to adapt to my schedule and that I was making things very inconvenient for her. Grace was far from the pleasant, outgoing, cooperative young woman whom I had met about a year ago. As she was reprimanding me, she sounded more like an army sergeant. Her voice was two octaves higher than usual, as she referred to me as "Strean" and as "one of those money-hungry shrinks." At one point she snarled, "I have little use for a schmuck like you."

As Grace discharged a great deal of hatred toward me, I had many mixed feelings. On one hand, I was pleased that she felt sufficiently safe with me that she could finally face the hurt and anger she had felt toward the father who constantly withdrew from her. On the other hand, a part of my narcissism was punctured. The loving daughter who I thought I had was no longer so loving. She hated my guts and it didn't feel too good. Nonetheless, my therapeutic ego for the most part was running the show and I tried to keep quiet and encourage Grace to express whatever she had to say about my vacation. I have found that when the therapist accepts and is non-judgmental about what the patient feels toward him or her, waits before making interpretations or other interventions, and if the patient is listened to without much overt response, the transference reactions help the patient recall memories. This is certainly what happened with Grace. She began to tell me how much I was just like her father— unavailable, unemotional, and uncaring. Grace had thought that she had in me "a different kind of father" but she was "wrong."

Until I went away on vacation, Grace spent almost all of her sessions talking about the unavailability of her father and how much she would have liked to depend on him. The bitterness and hurt that she expressed endured until the last session before our summer break. At the last session, Grace told me she wanted to "make up" with me. She realized that I was just taking a summer vacation I was entitled to, but it made her recall the many times she wanted to be with her father and, instead, felt rejected by him. Insightfully, she concluded, "I tended to take my father's absences and your absence much too personally. I don't think either of you was out to hurt me."

When I resumed work with Grace in the fall, she was glad to see me and I was happy to see her. She had had "a good August" and much of her life was going quite well. One item that struck me was that she had "nothing to do" with her mother over the summer. I wondered what my absence had stirred up in her vis-à-vis her mother and if her avoidance of her mother had something to do with an avoidance of some part of the maternal transference.

Hatred toward Her Mother

As is true with most patients most of the time, Grace's behavior in the therapy matched her behavior outside of it. She reported thoughts and feelings about all her current relationships, including her relationship with me, but Grace said nothing about her mother. It was almost as if her mother did not exist in her life.

I have often found it helpful to review periodically not only what patients have been telling me, but also to remind myself what they have not discussed. Some patients talk a great deal about the past, but leave out much of the present. Some talk a lot about sex, but can't discuss money. Many can talk about parents but omit references to siblings. A few can talk about everybody else in their lives except their therapists.

What a patient avoids discussing may be considered a message that the person and/or issue is fraught with anxiety. By avoiding the issue, the patient believes he or she can avoid facing painful affects and seemingly unsurmountable conflicts. It was with this in mind that I suggested to Grace in the early phase of her second year of treatment that I thought talking about her mother was quite painful to her. I further suggested that inasmuch as she felt it wasn't easy to talk to her father about her mother, maybe she felt similarly with me. To my surprise Grace said, "I was waiting for you to bring up my mother. I guess I needed your permission to do so. I think I've always felt that my mother was a taboo subject. I thought if my father didn't want to talk about her, it was wrong for me to talk about her."

As Grace and I discussed her relationship with her mother, it became very clear that it was a complex one. As far back as she could remember, she felt that her mother very much resented her and preferred her brother and sister. When family and friends referred to Grace's pretty appearance and charm, her mother demeaned her and often changed the subject. The more Grace grew into a tall, attractive young woman, the more her mother seemed threatened by her. When Grace became a teacher, her mother scoffed. When she dated boys, her mother either was contemptuous of the young men or acted seductively with them.

Toward the middle of her second year of therapy and for several months thereafter, Grace reported a number of dreams, all of which involved her mother. In several, mother was a witch trying to torment and physically harm Grace. In other dreams and fantasies there were oedipal themes in which Grace was trying to compete with her mother for father, or for other men. Grace would always end up being the loser.

Although Grace's death wishes toward, and her competition with her mother and fear of her retaliation became quite clear, it took us a while to really understand Grace's strong emotional investment in her mother and her futile battle with her.

Fortunately, toward the end of Grace's second year of treatment, she had a dream that gave a reasonably good clue as to what had sparked her intense and conflicted involvement with her mother. In the dream Grace was a little girl who couldn't find her way out of a big forest. As she "fretted, fussed, and fumed," and was close to giving herself up for lost or even dead, Grace met her mother, who was attempting to rescue her. In the dream, she felt an impulse to hug her mother but did not.

The dream clearly reflected how lonely and distressed Grace felt without her mother's love. It also showed that underneath her hatred, she yearned for her mother's love. When I suggested that one of the reasons she continued to feel very angry at her mother was because she could not forgive her mother for not loving and hugging her, Grace was very moved. Sobbing, she "had to confess" that what would change her life was knowing that she had a mother who loved her.

I have continued to believe that one of the major turning points in the therapy of the unattached is their getting in touch with their wish to love and be loved by their parents. Although this usually involves a difficult period of mourning, most patients would rather mourn a loss than go on hating. Hating usually constricts and leads to all kinds of unpleasant symptoms such as insomnia, headaches, and so forth. However, when the patient is aware that he or she wants to love and be loved, there is usually more freedom and less pain.

As Grace acknowledged her wish to capture her mother's love, she reported that she had not paid sufficient attention to the little girl inside her who wanted to be caressed, fondled, held, and adored. She tried, after achieving this insight, to get Gordon to gratify this wish and was quite successful.

Grace did not react as hostilely to the announcement of my summer vacation as she did the previous year. Rather, she was sad and wished that she could go on vacation with me.

A Surprising Development

Very often a therapist's absence clarifies dimensions of the transference of which neither the patient nor the therapist is aware. Many patients express their rage at the therapist for "abandoning" them by getting sicker and even threatening suicide. Some seek out a new relationship as a substitute for the therapist. Others displace their anger toward the therapist and do to others what they would like to do to the therapist.

During the summer vacation that followed her second year of therapy, Grace, to my surprise and others around her, ended her relationship with Gordon. As soon as she told me about this development, I intuitively sensed it had something to do with my absence. However, I had to wait to hear what Grace had to say about her decision.

At first, Grace had a matter-of-fact attitude about breaking off with Gordon. She said, "He had a limited income and therefore I would have limited pleasures living with him." As I listened carefully to Grace's productions, there was a shallowness to her affect and an emotional distance when she spoke to me.

Frequently when a patient makes a major decision and

does not involve the therapist, there is an unconscious wish to get rid of the therapist. Inasmuch as Grace had talked the previous summer of having nothing to do with her mother and had some wishes to get rid of her, I thought that unconsciously this might be taking place again. Further, Grace was very composed about my going away this time and I started to wonder whether I was now being experienced as the hated mother.

A technique I have found useful when I think the patient is unconsciously hating me but finding it difficult to confront me, is to make some references to myself and then study carefully what the patient does with this. When I asked Grace why she didn't want to talk over with me her decision to end her relationship with Gordon, her response clarified what was lying dormant in her transference.

The Negative Maternal Transference

Before I finished asking why she had not consulted me regarding breaking up with Gordon, Grace bellowed, "You think you are so damn important! Well, I don't think so! I broke off with him because I decided that was in my best interest, not in yours!"

Grace went on to tell me that I was a "highly narcissistic, self-involved shrink" who did not really care too much about my patients' welfare because I was mainly interested in my vacation and my income. Although I was aware that Grace was experiencing me now as the hateful mother of her past, I felt that it would not be helpful to say anything about this for a while. She needed to bring out all of the hatred she could never express to her mother. I hoped if I empathetically listened and said little, after discharging what she had to discharge she would see what she was reexperiencing.

For several months I thought that Grace would go on hating me for the rest of her life. I had discovered over the years that there are some patients who get more pleasure acting out revenge than turning their lives around (Strean 1993) and I was worried Grace might be one of them. However, one difference in the outcome of a case where the patient has a strong negative therapeutic reaction is the therapist's own countertransference (Searles 1979). If the therapist does not feel too retaliatory toward the patient, the patient usually senses this. I did not hate Grace and at the most felt irritated with her from time to time. Consequently, I both hoped and thought that our working alliance might serve Grace to begin to master her hatred.

After mocking me, demeaning me, and belittling me for most of her third year in therapy, Grace had a very revealing insight. In April of that year, Grace said confidently, "I've noticed that as I go on hating you, I can't love a man." After Grace went on to reflect more about this insight, I was able to interpret to her that just as it was difficult to give up hating her mother, it was difficult to give up hating me.

Working Through

During Grace's fourth year of her twice-weekly therapy, she spent a great deal of her time trying to understand better what motivated her to hang on to her hatred of her mother. She knew that she felt very revengeful for all of the hurts she had endured and was also aware of the fact that by winning an oedipal victory, she could humiliate her mother, much the way she had felt humiliated by her.

What we learned during this period was that Grace experienced her anger toward her mother as a sign of strength—as a useful weapon. When I asked her what would happen if she did not hold onto her weapon (which she eventually labeled "a sword"), she talked about feeling very vulnerable. "I would be the little girl of my past who wanted mother's love but got crushed instead," Grace declared.

When Grace saw that she equated receiving love with being a vulnerable little girl, she began to feel more liberated. She saw that whenever she was receiving love, she had a tendency to turn the other person into a combination of her father (who was withdrawn) and her mother (who was hostile and rejecting). Seeing this distortion helped Grace feel more womanly and more maternal, particularly in her relationships with men.

As Grace felt more "adult-like," she moved into a new relationship with another man, Perry. Perry was an attorney, several years older than Grace, who was very "giving, supportive, and clear-headed." In her sexual relationship with Perry, Grace reported that she did not have to compete with her mother as much and, consequently, she derived much more pleasure. After dating for about seven months, Grace and Perry decided to live together. After one year, they were married.

Termination

Shortly after Perry and Grace decided to live together, Grace felt that she could consider ending treatment. Although she expressed a lot of sadness and some anger that there would no longer be "a comforting mother and father" in her life, Grace felt that Perry would be "a very gratifying partner." We spent about four or five months discussing termination. Grace worried that in missing me, she might "become a sad and vulnerable little girl" again. When I interpreted that ending treatment rekindled emotional separation from both her parents, Grace guessed a part of her would always want to retreat to the position of "a needy daughter."

One issue that we did not fully resolve during the termination phase was that Grace wanted me to attend her wedding and I did not consent. My position with Grace, as it is with all patients, is not to say "yes" or "no" when I'm invited, but to help the patients verbalize what it means to have me at the wedding. Mostly, there is a wish for me to be a benign superego and sanction the marriage. Sometimes there is a lingering wish that I be the groom and by attending the wedding, I become a symbolic groom.

When Grace explored why she wanted me to attend the wedding, she had fantasies of me dancing a waltz with her. At first she fantasized I would be "the father of the bride," and later she had fantasies of marrying me. I recalled that she had had a dream early in treatment in which we were dancing together.

Grace, although disappointed and somewhat angry that I analyzed with her her wish to have me at the wedding rather than gratifying her desire, gave the reason I do not attend weddings of patients better than I have ever stated it. She said, "I sometimes forget that you are my therapist. If you are at the wedding, it will appear at least that day that you and I are something else beside patient and therapist. I guess it's my wish to continue to be your daughter or wife or young sister."

Grace did enjoy her wedding and her marriage as well. Each Christmas I receive a card from her reporting on her "enjoyable and productive life with Perry." Perry and Grace had two children during the first four years of their marriage. From every indication it would appear that her marriage and family life is a mutually loving one. Clearly she is enjoying her attachment.

5

The Case of Kevin Morton

A barely audible voice at the other end of the phone greeted me on a late Friday afternoon, just as I was leaving my office for the weekend. It was difficult to decipher the words of the person calling, and I didn't know whether it was a man or woman. The voice murmured hesitantly, "My name is Kevin Morton. I would like to make an appointment with you . . . to discuss my situation. . . . Your name was given to me by my doctor who said my headaches, backaches, and insomnia are due to psychological factors."

As I strained to listen to Kevin Morton, I heard a voice that sounded in pain, and I found myself feeling sorry for Kevin even though I had not met him. He seemed very morose and induced in me a strong wish to reach out to him. I told him I could meet with him the following Monday. "I can come to your office after I finish school. I teach and I can get to your office after 4 PM," he responded.

When I went into the waiting room at the designated time, I saw a man about 5 feet 11 inches tall, in his late thirties, very thin, with baggy trousers and a jacket that was ragged and not in fashion. His clothes matched his expression; he looked haggard and obviously very depressed. Actually, he was quite unkempt. His glasses were broken and dirty, his hair uncombed, and his shoes muddy.

After we entered the consultation room and I showed Kevin where he could sit, he looked at me deferentially but was silent. I broke the silence after about ten seconds and told Kevin that he had informed me over the phone that he was having some physical problems. Perhaps he could tell me some more about these problems?

In the same depressed, halting monotone that I had heard over the phone, Kevin mentioned that for the past three years he had not slept well and had many different bodily aches and pains including migraines. When I observed that Kevin did not link his somatic difficulties to anything psychological, I tried to see if he had done any thinking along these lines, so I asked, "Was there anything going on in your life three years ago that might have been difficult to cope with?" Kevin went into a thoughtful silence and after about twenty seconds said with a pained expression, "It was about three years ago that my wife left me and then divorced me." "Oh, how come?" I asked.

Kevin told me that he and his wife Mary had been married for five years. According to Kevin, Mary was dissatisfied with him from the beginning of their marriage. He was too shy, too sloppy, a poor lover, a poor conversationalist—he didn't have anything positive going for him.

When I wondered how Kevin felt to be in a relationship in which he was constantly being criticized, he responded tersely, "It wasn't very good." Then he went into a long silence. During the silence, I found myself reflecting on some thoughts and feelings I was having about Kevin. Although his depression was obvious from his dress, speech, and lack of emotional spontaneity, I felt he was quite unrelated. When I sensed traces of irritation in myself because Kevin was so hard to reach, after censuring myself for them it occurred to me that Kevin must have frustrated his wife Mary in the way I was feeling frustrated. Because Kevin had so much of his affect under enormous control, I wondered how much aggression he had buried. As I reflected on his marriage, I was puzzled about what brought these people together—they seemed so far apart.

Realizing that my irritation in the session stemmed from Kevin being so ungiving with regard to his emotions and thoughts, I began to consider how unsafe he must be feeling and I conjectured that this might be what he had experienced in many relationships. "Maybe," I wondered to myself, "he drives lots of people away." I then reminded myself that he probably felt lonely, isolated, and unloved most of the time.

While I was silently talking to myself, I was suddenly startled. I became aware that after being with each other for only a short while, we had spent the last four minutes in silence. I quickly queried, "May I ask what you are feeling now?" "I'm okay," he responded tersely. "What thoughts and feelings were you having during the silence?" I asked. "Nothing," Kevin answered.

The fifteen minutes or so that I had been with Kevin seemed like three hours. I was getting more and more restless and felt that Kevin and I were not really communicating. I knew I was feeling angry because, as I mentioned in a previous chapter, whenever I start using diagnostic labels like "schizoid" or "borderline," I know I am participating in what Erikson (1950) dubbed "diagnostic name-calling." I thought, "This guy is feeling miserable. You can't expect him to give you very much. If you expect a lot from him, you'll drive him and you crazy! You'll have to ask him questions and be prepared for short answers." Once I lowered my expectations, the rest of the interview with Kevin went reasonably well. I decided to ask him more about his relationship with Mary. One of the issues that interested me was their courtship and whether Mary was dissatisfied with Kevin from the very beginning.

It turned out that Mary was the school nurse in a junior high school where Kevin was a mathematics teacher. Kevin routinely went to the nurse's office because he often suffered from nausea, headaches, colds, and other somatic difficulties. Mary obviously enjoyed ministering to a sick man, and although Kevin was not consciously aware of it at the time, I clearly sensed he welcomed having someone take care of him or "nurse" him.

From the early beginnings of their relationship, Kevin appeared to be Mary's project. She nurtured him, doctored him, tried to make a man out of him, but seemed to be exasperated by his lack of progress. Consciously Kevin tried to comply with Mary's rules and regulations but he was clearly defying her by dressing like a slob, showing very limited sexual or emotional initiative, and appearing withdrawn much of the time.

When I could feel some clarity about Kevin's marital interaction, I began to inquire about his history. I learned that Kevin came from an Irish-Catholic family. His father was a laborer who had a meager education and was unemployed much of the time. In addition, he was a withdrawn man who watched television a lot and was often drunk. Kevin expressed a thinly veiled contempt toward his father. Kevin's mother ran the family. Similar to the way Mary appeared, the mother was very dominant, controlling, and symbiotic. She tried very hard to get Kevin to become what her husband was not—an educated and competent man. She herself had also a limited formal education. Kevin clearly tried to please his mother by becoming a teacher, but it was evident that he resented being compliant.

Kevin had a sister who was eight years younger than he. Kevin told me that because he was so much older than

his sister, he did not have much to do with her. At the
time of the initial consultation, his sister lived in the
Southwest.

In the second half of the first session, Kevin continued
to answer my questions tersely and with little affect. I
learned that he was never better than an average student
in high school and college, never had many friends, and
enjoyed his hobby of collecting coins. In the school where
he taught, the students and he "got along all right," but he
did have difficulty from time to time maintaining discipline.

Kevin decided to start therapy on a weekly basis. He
told me that he would be able to afford my usual fee
because, he assured me, "the insurance will take care of 80
percent of it."

The Initial Interviews

Kevin came on time for his weekly interviews. He never
appeared enthusiastic or well motivated, but dutifully
answered my questions with unemotional, not very revealing answers. As I observed my interaction with Kevin,
I began to realize that it was similar to the interaction he
had described with his mother and former wife. On the
surface he tried to comply and give me what he thought I
wanted. However, it was clear that Kevin was not enjoying our relationship and probably was holding back a
great deal of resentment. After a few months of work with
Kevin, I concluded that many of his psychosomatic symp-

toms were an expression of his deep resentment. Further, I felt a strong desire to help him release some of his repressed rage, which was contributing toward making him an emotional cripple.

Working on Kevin's Rage

I knew that to help Kevin face his pent-up hostility would not be an easy task. I speculated that he probably would want to please me, but would also want to fight me. In the end I thought there was a good chance he would try to sabotage my efforts. But, I wanted to try to reach him.

I started my project (much as Mary and his mother had turned their efforts with Kevin into projects) by asking him how he felt about our work so far. In his characteristic manner, he responded, "All right." He used the same two words, "all right," to describe how he felt in the sessions and how he felt toward me. Although I gave myself an A for my initial efforts, my initial results were worth an F or D minus.

In the past when I was confronted with a very resistant and stubborn patient like Kevin, I occasionally disclosed some of my countertransference reactions to the patient (Strean, 1991, 1993). This can diminish some of the on-going tension for me, and, in addition, the patient has the opportunity to experience me as a real person with real feelings and vulnerabilities. This makes me appear more like my patient experiences himself or herself and less of an authoritarian parental figure who is out to dominate and control the patient. With this in mind, I disclosed some of my countertransference feelings to Kevin.

I told Kevin that from the first time I met him until now, I was trying to help him and that he was trying very hard to comply with my requests. He was coming on time, paying on time, and trying his best to answer my questions. I also thought that, as with his mother and with Mary, he resented my demands on him but found it very difficult to tell me about his anger. I also told him I had been trying hard to help him talk about his anger, but that he was successfully defeating me and I felt like a loser!

For the first time in the four months, I saw him crack a smile! This warmed the cockles of my heart and I sensed that he knew this. Kevin then made his most insightful and longest statement since I knew him. "I never liked obeying rules, yet everywhere I go I'm always looking for them. Sometimes I think I look for rules so that I can break them. I'm glad you know this about me!"

Kevin came in the following week to say that he had "the best week" he had in years. He slept every night, did not have his usual stomach pains and headaches, and decided to have his first date since his divorce. I felt elated on hearing this.

The Honeymoon Phase

Soon after Kevin saw that his painful symptoms diminished and that he was feeling much better, he started to dress with more care and relate to me and others with much less detachment. He increased the frequency of his sessions all on his own initiative. Also on his own initiative, Kevin began to take a look at his relationships with his family and to see how these relationships influenced his current self-image and interactions with others. He pointed out that he had a very distant relationship with his father, and, with much difficulty, told me that he could not respect him very much. His father was not literate, was asleep much of the time in front of the television set, and had no interest in anything substantial with the possible exception of baseball.

During Kevin's eighth month of treatment while talking fairly animatedly about his father, he suddenly stopped talking and went into a long silence. When I tried to investigate what Kevin was feeling during the silence, he remained silent. Usually this sort of event in psychotherapy suggests an uncomfortable transference reaction taking place below the surface. Therefore, I suggested, "Perhaps you are having some feelings toward me while you are talking to me about your father." After another silence of about fifteen seconds, Kevin began to sob. Then he told me he wished he had me for a father. He would have felt valued by a man he respected and this would have helped him gain some self-respect.

In a dream he had at this time, Kevin made himself a young boy and was playing baseball with me, his coach. He could interpret the dream himself, telling me that he wanted me to help him become more manly by being a warm father figure to him. As Kevin felt closer to me, he began to date women with some regularity. He found himself more at ease sexually and was more potent than he ever had been. Kevin stated at the end of his ninth month in treatment, "I'm riding high!"

A Treatment Crisis

At the beginning of Kevin's tenth month of therapy, he declared that he had derived a great deal from his work with me and felt ready to terminate treatment. Although I felt he had made many gains, I also believed that Kevin had some further work to do. Despite his having faced certain facets of his relationship with his father, I believed there were some unresolved conflicts that needed further examination. Of equal, if not more importance, Kevin had not discussed his relationship with his mother very much and I was convinced that before he could really enjoy a relationship with a woman, he needed to face his ambivalence toward his mother. Further, inasmuch as Kevin was interested in leaving me, I was quite convinced that he was once again avoiding facing certain painful transference reactions.

Because there was no possibility of our working on his unresolved conflicts if he left, I decided to work on the transference first. (I have contended for some time that when a patient wants to leave a therapist, it is best to give the negative transference priority, because any discussion will be shaped by it.)

I asked Kevin how he felt about not seeing me anymore. Kevin went into a long silence. Having now experienced several of his prolonged silences, I had a reasonably good idea about their dynamic meaning. I said, "Usually when you are very quiet, you have feelings toward me that are difficult to talk about." At first, Kevin said he wasn't aware of any feelings toward me, but he did think he would miss our sessions when he quit. After another long silence, Kevin remarked, "I know I'm uncomfortable about being with you but I don't know why."

I told Kevin that I, too, wasn't sure what was making him uncomfortable, but I was very curious. I suggested that his discomfort seemed to have emerged after he was feeling quite close to me and had some fantasies about my being his father. Kevin balked at any further discussion about my being a father figure. Actually he became indignant and told me it was foolish for him to entertain fantasies that could never be fulfilled. He averred, "One should forget about wishes that can't be gratified."

As I listened carefully to Kevin's protests, I was able to make an interpretation. I told him that the wish to have me as his father—which was understandable—was something he wanted to fight. By leaving me, he wouldn't have to face it. Again, Kevin disagreed and reiterated his notion that he had derived a great deal from his therapy and was ready to quit.

What was now occurring with Kevin was an event that all therapists experience many times and to which I alluded earlier. When a patient is in a negative transference, he or she is going to respond negatively to almost anything the therapist says (Strean 1991). Consequently, the accuracy or truth of an interpretation is not the sine qua non of its acceptance by the patient. Inaccurate and untruthful interpretations will tend to be accepted by a patient who is in a positive transference, and accurate and truthful statements will tend to be rejected by a patient who is in a negative transference.

It did not surprise me that Kevin rejected my interpretation since it was important for him at this juncture to reject me. When I pointed out that it was very important to him to create distance between us, and therefore he had to disagree with me, Kevin responded with, "I disagree with that too!" We both laughed when I said, "See what I mean!"

Having fought me for several weeks and seeing I was not going to counterattack or agree to a termination, Kevin began to be less defiant and stubborn. Furthermore, because there was a part of him that did want to continue the relationship Kevin did modify his position by saying, "I think you want me to stay in treatment, so I'll listen to you—you're the expert."

Though I did want him to stay in therapy, I did not feel comfortable about his doing so in order to please me. This is what he did with Mary and with his mother—please them and hate doing so. I said, "Sometimes I think it is easier for you to please others than to please yourself." Kevin agreed and said that this was a pattern of behavior that he had used for many years.

The Ambivalent Paternal Transference

As we investigated his wish to placate others, we learned that Kevin had many death wishes toward his father but felt very guilty and anxious about them. To deny and repress his competition and contempt toward his father and others, he did the opposite—became ingratiating and compliant. What he did was an excellent illustration of the defense called *reaction formation*.

Kevin was eventually able to tell me that as much as he enjoyed his relationship with me, it also bothered him because while gaining pleasure from our work he was secretly telling his father to "go to hell." Kevin pointed out, "If I tell myself that you, Herb Strean, are my good father, I feel as if my own father is being thrown away and that makes me feel like an ingrate."

Kevin also realized that as he was feeling stronger and more competent, he was worried that he would not only topple his father, but was frightened that he would surpass me in "many areas."

I felt that if Kevin could work more on some of his phallic-oedipal issues, it would help him feel a lot more comfortable in his relationships with the opposite sex. Therefore, I wanted to encourage him to feel more relaxed about surpassing me in "many areas." I suggested, "Let's look at some of the areas when you may have already surpassed me. I think it can be helpful." Although Kevin had some reluctance to share those thoughts, he was eventually able to tell me that he was taller, stronger, and more masculine than I. He also reminded me that he was a very competent mathematician and he "kind of doubted" I knew as much math as he did. With a little bit of help Kevin could share with me that he thought a lot of young women would be more attracted to him than they would be to me.

In my response, I emphasized that what Kevin referred to were not mere fantasies. Realistically, he was taller, stronger, and younger than I. He certainly knew a lot more about mathematics, and with all these real assets I was sure young women would be more attracted to him.

Kevin turned red as a beet. He told me he was "very uncomfortable" showing me up, and then raising his voice said, "When I think of surpassing you, I feel I'm turning you into a nobody like my father was."

Kevin's conviction that he could turn his father or me into a nobody was something we worked on for a couple of months. He needed help in coming to grips with the fact that though he might have wished to turn us into nobodies, that is, kill us, did not mean that he was as powerful as he would have liked. What Kevin had to confront, in effect, were intense grandiose and omnipotent fantasies. These fantasies had been unconscious virtually all of his life and had influenced much of his behavior.

Facing his strong oedipal fantasies helped Kevin immensely. What he could really appreciate was how and why he defended against these fantasies. His deferential attitude toward me, his masochistic surrender to Mary, his submissive attitude toward his mother, his inability to take too much initiative with women, were all mechanisms to avoid facing the murderous wishes that terrified him. They terrified him because he was afraid he would act them out and therefore become a sadistic killer.

The Ambivalent Maternal Transference

By the middle of his third year in therapy, Kevin was much less depressed and was working and loving with more pleasure. Although he was dating women and feeling more confident with them, he was not in a sustained, intimate relationship. Because of this void in his life, I believed he still needed further therapeutic work.

When I asked Kevin if he had some desire to have a close, continuing relationship with one woman, he responded affirmatively. At this point in our work he was able to associate to this problem without much anxiety. He pointed out that he often found himself thinking that the closer he got to a woman, the more he feared being dominated and controlled by her, the way Mary and his mother had done. What Kevin was not aware of was his own unconscious wish to be a little boy with a woman and turn her into a mother figure. Although relieved to discover that women just didn't dominate him but that he had a role in influencing the process, it did not answer the question, "Why do I want women to mother me?"

We learned that the wish to turn women into mothers was an overdetermined wish. First, Kevin realized that he enjoyed the passivity and lack of responsibility in keeping himself a young boy. Second, by keeping himself a boy, he did not have to worry about surpassing his father and others—he was only a boy. Finally, as a boy who related to women as if they were preoedipal mothers, Kevin did not have to think of himself as a sexual person. He could avoid facing his incestuous fantasies.

Many aspects of Kevin's conflicts with his mother emerged in his transference to me. In a dream he had during this period, he arranged for me to feed him and then wipe his behind. In another dream, he arranged for me to encourage him to read a book. This was what his mother did constantly when he was a young boy.

When I observed that Kevin consistently made himself into a young boy with me and also continued to make me the dominating preoedipal mother, I began to wonder why he needed this defense so much. Asking Kevin about this, he eventually informed me, "To be a big guy with the old lady made me feel like her lover." And then laughing, Kevin commented, "It's not easy, you know, to be a mother fucker."

Working Through and Termination

As Kevin was resolving both the paternal and maternal transference—not opposing his father as much and not being so dominated by his mother—he became more self-confident and much less masochistic and depressed. Of crucial importance, he began to date one woman exclusively. His girlfriend, Jane, was a social worker who was also finishing her own personal therapy and therefore the two of them had that in common.

From time to time while dating Jane, Kevin tried to provoke her into becoming the controlling mother, but she was not too willing to comply. On other occasions, he tried to engage me into competing for Jane but recognized that this undertaking was a futile battle. By the time Kevin had been in therapy four years, he was ready to terminate. He had some difficulty separating from me, contending that I was both the father and mother he had always wanted. However, Jane was giving him so much gratification that the pain of separation was eased.

I have heard from Kevin indirectly over the years since he ended therapy. He has referred colleagues and friends to me for treatment, who have all spoken highly of him and of his good relationship with Jane.

6

The Case of
Alice Peterson

When I entered the waiting room, I saw a matronly looking woman in rather drab clothes who appeared to be in her late forties or early fifties. She wore large-framed eyeglasses and was so absorbed in reading a technical computer journal that she did not hear me enter the room. Alice Peterson, who turned out to be a 52-year-old computer analyst, smiled meekly after hearing me say, "Hello, Ms. Peterson" for the third time. Realizing I had been in the room for almost a minute, Ms. Peterson apologized profusely and said, "I lost myself in my reading."

Referred by a former patient of mine, Ms. Peterson opened the interview by referring to her friend Joan, and said, "Joan persuaded me to come here." I immediately responded to the word "persuaded" and commented, "Oh, you aren't sure you want to be here?" Alice said, "Well, you see, I've been in all kinds of therapy for over twenty years. I've had individual therapy, group therapy, sex therapy, and other treatment, and nothing has helped me very much. I've been wanting to get married for close to thirty years and I haven't been very successful." In addition to feeling uncomfortable being "a fifth wheel," and a "social misfit," Alice informed me that for most of her adult life she suffered from acute and chronic constipation, constant insomnia, severe migraine headaches, and frequent heart palpitations.

As I listened to Alice's presentation, I clearly detected her thinly veiled resistance to becoming involved in further therapy. She had to be "persuaded" to see me and she had "all kinds of therapy," none of which was very helpful. Further, many of her symptoms were of long-standing duration, which I conjectured had to make her doubt how much psychotherapy could help her.

I felt that Alice's ambivalent motivation toward treatment needed discussion. I had heard about and seen many men and women who had had many years of unproductive therapy, but their weak motivation had never been addressed in the therapy. Rather, their fears of revealing their doubts about treatment were covered over by a passive compliance that fooled the therapists who were only too eager to try to help them. I have learned that when therapists do not deal with a patient's opposition to therapy, the treatment can drag on for years without much being accomplished.

With the aforementioned in mind, I said to Alice Peterson, "As I learn of how much time, energy, and money you've spent on psychotherapy and haven't gotten that much out of it, I think before you embark on another therapeutic journey, it might be helpful to talk over the pros and cons of it." Alice then looked somewhat surprised and thoughtfully said, "You know, I've never really thought about whether therapy is good or bad for me. I've just done it. I think I've done a lot of things that way. I tend to comply without thinking."

I wondered how Alice's latent resentment toward therapy could have escaped four or five therapists, and I felt that this issue would be a good thing to discuss with her as soon as I could. Therefore, I asked, "Do you have any thoughts about why your doubts about therapy didn't get discussed with your previous therapists?" Alice informed me that all of her life she had been "a good girl" and always did what she thought was expected of her. I asked, "Without always considering what you felt about the demands being made on you?" "You got it," Alice responded with a smile.

Alice went on to tell me that although she had been in therapy for many years, she had not considered until now "the inescapable fact" that she has always tended to believe that what the expert says or does is right. "The expert is infallible," Alice said with amusement and a touch of sarcasm. As we were talking about Alice's strong tendency to submit to authorities, I asked her about her parents. With much reverence she spoke of her father who was a well-known federal judge. "He was a kind man but very exacting," Alice reflected. "He made me and my younger sister believe that we should always be ladies. We weren't supposed to say very much but we were always to be respectful." As Alice described her father in more detail, it became quite clear that she experienced him as a very punitive superego who was against any expression of sexuality and aggression. He insisted that Alice and her sister Gwen should never walk around the house in slips, should only attend events with boys that were chaperoned, and should never use any curse words.

It was while talking about her father that Alice mentioned she could almost "count on the fingers of one hand" the number of men with whom she had had sex. Although she could derive some pleasure from her sexual and interpersonal contacts with men, she could not quite understand why virtually every man she dated had left her prematurely.

The discomfort that Alice experienced with men became a vicious cycle. By her late teens she was so worried about her dates dropping her that she became tongue-tied in her conversations with men. Sensing her resistance to contact, the men would move away. Alice told me that despite all of her therapy experiences, this pattern never was altered.

Although Gwen experienced her father the same way Alice did, she dated much more than Alice and was married twice. Despite the fact that both marriages ended in divorce, Gwen was much freer sexually than Alice and derived much more pleasure from men. Alice told me she was envious of Gwen because of her ability to sustain relationships with men and also because she had two children whom she enjoyed and who loved her.

Noting that Alice had not mentioned anything about her mother, I asked about her. Alice's mother (and father) died when she was in her late twenties. Mother was described as a very quiet woman who was very subordinate to Alice's father and who did not seem to have much of a role in the family's life.

As our interview was coming to a close, Alice inquired, "Do you think I should go into treatment with you now?" I told Alice I realized this was a difficult decision for her. I further mentioned that one thing I had already learned about her was a tendency to defer to the expert or authority and permit her own wishes to go underground. Alice responded, "So you don't think you should make the decision for me?" "Do you?" I asked. "Well, it would be a lot easier for me," Alice retorted. After a silence, Alice asked if it would be permissible to have another consultation and then make a decision. I told her it might be helpful to talk a little more and maybe that would help her make a firmer decision about resuming therapy.

Before we ended the interview, I learned from Alice that she had a senior position in a large computer company. She liked her work, got along well with most people there "except some individuals in authority," had saved quite a bit of money, owned an apartment she "adored," and had several close women friends.

When I reflected on my interview with Alice, I was essentially pleased with it. I was glad that I had gotten in touch with her opposition to therapy, which she defended against by adopting a deferential and compliant attitude. This helped me hypothesize that a part of her was still at war with her father and all men and that this war kept her from a close relationship with a man. I was also pleased that I could see how this conflict was played out in her previous therapy with both male and female therapists. I cautioned myself not to be seduced by her ingratiating attitude the way my colleagues had been.

I know that therapeutic work with Alice would not be easy and that if I were to help her, she and I would have to deal with and live through a negative transference.

The Initial Interviews

It was no surprise to either Alice or me that after her initial consultation she would want to continue her contact with me. Although her compliant attitude certainly was a crucial factor in determining her decision, I also thought that a certain amount of hope emerged from her initial interview. Sensing that I could relate to her compliant defense and get in touch with some of her latent resentment gave Alice another, and perhaps more hopeful, way to view her problems.

Reuben Fine (1982) in *The Healing of the Mind* pointed out that one of the most important variables that induces the prospective patient to decide to enter treatment and stay there is hope. If the therapist conducts himself or herself in a way that suggests to the patient that there is something to look at that will improve the prospective patient's life, she will usually stay in treatment. Although other variables, such as strong resistances, poor motivation, negative transference, negative countertransference, or severe pathology in the patient and/or the therapist, of course, influence the outcome of therapy, hope always springs eternal!

It was also not a surprise that Alice always came to her sessions on time, paid on time, and overtly seemed like a most cooperative patient. She could easily talk about dreams, fantasies, history, and emotions in what appeared to be a productive manner. Yet, as I carefully listened to Alice and concomitantly examined my own emotional responses, more and more I sensed there was something missing. I began to empathize with Alice's previous therapists who, I believed, wanted to help her and thought they were doing so but Alice's modus vivendi did not change appreciably.

It was during Alice's fourth month of her twice-a-week treatment that it dawned on me what the void was all about. Despite Alice's overt cooperation, whatever she felt toward me and about me was not being discussed; she had a strong resistance to sharing her transference responses. As I thought further about that, it occurred to me that it was not dissimilar from her way of relating to men generally. She was a cooperative lady who tried to be a well-behaved girl, but could not emotionally relate to the man. Therefore, in her transference relationship with me and in her interaction with men, Alice was "Daddy's Little Girl," complying with what she thought he wanted but never letting him know what she was feeling toward him or desired from him.

When many sessions go by and patients are not expressing transference reactions, I usually work with this resistance by gently asking them what they are feeling as they are talking. If this does not yield very much, in a subsequent session I might ask them what they are feeling toward me as they are talking. And, if this intervention is not helpful, I now have enough data to offer an interpretation.

When I went though the above procedure with Alice—and got nowhere—I was able to tell her that just as I felt she fought her feelings when with a man, this is what I thought she was doing with me. Alice did not like my interpretation, and my intervention provoked a strong negative transference reaction

The Negative Transference

In response to my interpretation, Alice became tearful and told me I was not appreciating how hard she was working in the therapy and that I did not seem satisfied with her efforts. She likened what was transpiring between us to her relationships with men where she always tried to please them but they became dissatisfied with her and left. When I suggested to Alice that it must feel quite discouraging to try hard to please me (and others) and then feel rebuked, she lamented, "This is the way it's always been. I was always a good girl wherever I went, and nobody seemed that pleased with me."

On my asking her what she thought displeased me about her, with some anger in her voice, she said, "You want me to talk about you, and I'm not doing that. I guess I'm not doing the work of this course." I pointed out to Alice that she seemed to feel like a student in a class trying to please me, rather than feeling she was my equal and that we were trying to resolve something together.

Alice then went on to tell me that she never felt she was any man's equal. Consequently, she had "to please," "to ingratiate," "to defer," and never talk about her own wishes, or likes and dislikes. As she became more sensitized to her compliant attitudes, she slowly began to realize that throughout her life she had been in a rage against the whole world. She resented her father for insisting on her being an asexual, compliant girl. She resented her mother for not helping her become a sexual woman. She resented her sister for being able to have men and sex while she couldn't. And she resented the men she dated for giving her next to nothing while she gave them her all.

It was when Alice was venting rage toward almost everybody in her life that I asked what it was about me that induced anger. Thoughtful at first, Alice went on to tell me, "You sit there like a knowing god, passing judgment on me. You show such little warmth but a lot of coldness. You like your work but you don't like me."

As I listened carefully to Alice's criticisms, I realized I was being portrayed as the cold, exacting judge her father appeared to be. I also thought that she needed help in feeling safe in expressing that resentment without any interference on my part.

Slowly Alice began to have dreams and fantasies in which she maimed me, castrated me, and then demolished me. In one dream she made herself into a witch and enjoyed mocking me and kicking me while I fell to the ground, and she laughed. She was doing to me in the transference what all masochistic patients want to do— become a sadist and have the therapist suffer they way they did.

A Dramatic Development

In her ninth month of therapy there was a new development. She confessed that for over fifteen years, because of her chronic constipation, she had to spend two hours every night giving herself enemas. Aside from the time and inconvenience involved, Alice always worried that no man would tolerate this.

What helped her feel extremely elated was that for the past few weeks (when she began to discharge her rage in therapy), she had been able to move her bowels normally. At first, Alice could not find any particular reason to account for the great improvement in her gastrointestinal functioning. However, toward the end of her first year of treatment, she had a dream in which she was throwing mud pies at me. She did not need too much help in saying, "I'd really like to throw shit at you."

The Intense Oedipal Conflict

Alice's severe gastrointestinal problems could be regarded as a profound regression. Unable to cope with her sexual fantasies toward her father and her competitive feelings toward her mother and sister, Alice became preoccupied with anal matters. Her constipation was an overdetermined symptom. Not only did the regression move her away from the anxiety that her sexual fantasies induced, but she could also get some masturbatory gratification in daily inserting an enema stick up her anus. In addition, the rage that Alice repressed toward men and women, which was repugnant to her, could be controlled symbolically by being constipated.

When Alice had released a great deal of hostility and her constipation disappeared entirely, her transference toward me also changed dramatically. She began to feel very grateful toward me and had many loving fantasies. She increased the frequency of her sessions to three times a week and began to feel a real conviction that her therapy could help her. Alice's loving wishes toward me started to include sexual fantasies. She had numerous dreams and fantasies in which she was vacationing with me, dancing with me, and eventually having sex with me. However, there was a lot of anxiety and hesitancy attached to her expression of libidinal wishes and I attempted to focus on this resistance.

A dream that Alice had in her fourteenth month of treatment involved the two of us on a vacation, relaxing in a hotel room. In the dream, while she was reading an article that I was writing, I angrily grabbed the article from her hand, refused to let her read it, and told her, "Mind your own business."

As we tried to understand my anger in the dream, at first Alice could only say that I wanted to reject her. However, when I reminded Alice that she was the one who wrote the script of her dream and therefore there had to be some reason why she arranged to be rejected by me, Alice had a very helpful insight. She began to recall how much her father was against her being with young men and, therefore, would have been against her relationship with me. By having me angry at her, Alice could preserve her relationship with her father and, in effect, get rid of me.

By the time Alice was in the middle of her second year of treatment, she could definitely appreciate that she had kept herself away from men. She realized that if she allowed herself pleasure with men, her father would be angry at her. What was very important for Alice to understand was that her reluctance to have an intimate relationship with a man was an internalized conflict.

Despite the fact that Alice reminded herself continually that her parents were dead and realistically could not affect her relationship with me or with other men, she had constant dreams and fantasies of her parents punishing her for being intimately involved with a man. She saw clearly how very exacting her own punitive superego was.

As Alice discussed how much punishment she felt she deserved for being with and enjoying a man, it began to dawn on her that not only did she experience her father as not wanting her to love any man other than him, but that she felt the same way. "I do not want to love any man but my father. I want to be his lover," said Alice with much passion.

Reflecting more on her relationship with her father, Alice began to report fantasies of living with him, marrying him, and having a baby with him. It was during this time that I learned that most of the men she had sexual relations with were already married. Although Alice tried to believe that befriending married men was just a happenstance, she did not require much help in seeing that they were father figures for her.

Competition with Women

When Alice could acknowledge her wish to have her father all to herself, she felt much freer to date men and enjoy them. Not having to fight her incestuous wishes as much, she could see the men for who they were, not fathers who had to be avoided lest she "be considered a criminal," but men whom she could enjoy and could enjoy her.

As Alice began dating more but not married men, despite her pleasure in her "new life," there was something "gnawing" at her. What we eventually learned was that Alice wanted to continue to see her dates as fathers who were "stolen" from mothers. She had many fantasies and dreams of women reclaiming the men she was dating.

Alice had to face the joy she derived from winning a man from a woman. No sooner did she try to monitor her fantasies and see her dates more realistically, than she would turn to fantasies in which she would be taking her father from her mother and/or sister.

As is true for most conflicts, they have to be resolved in the transference relationship with the therapist. Into her third year of three-times-a week treatment, Alice talked about wishes of "grabbing" me away from my wife and from my other women patients and having me all to herself. When she did not receive any encouragement from me, she often became quite furious. Because I tried to stay neutral in the face of her fury, eventually she could face the futility of "being angry at a guy who is not mine."

Working Through and Termination

Alice had to spend four years in therapy trying to diminish her hatred toward her family members. Not only did she have to learn to forgive her father for being a squelching and unappreciative man, but of equal, if not more, importance, Alice had to accept the fact that he would not be her lover, nor would I. Alice also had to learn to like herself enough so that she did not need to prove herself to herself, nor to outdo her mother and sister as well as my female patients. These were tough jobs but she slowly began to recognize that if she were to love and be loved by a man, she couldn't be Daddy's lover and mother and sister's opponent at the same time.

Toward the end of Alice's fourth year of treatment, she

had an exclusive relationship with a widower, Art. Although they maintained separate residences, they spent a lot of time with each other which was mutually pleasureful.

Terminating therapy was difficult for Alice and for me. Alice kept trying to find rationales to continue her treatment, even though they masked her wish to make me her boyfriend. Because I was eager to see Alice with a man in a mature relationship, at times I tended to rush her through the termination phase. As is true with any patient, when Alice was rushed, she became more relentless in her wish to stay in treatment.

After four years, Alice was in a close, intimate, and enjoyable relationship with Art. They spend a good part of their week and every vacation together. I have heard from her several times since she formally terminated her therapy and she continues to adapt very well.

7

The Case of Ben Goldsmith

The polite voice on my telephone answering machine said, "This is Mr. Ben Goldsmith's secretary. Mr. Goldsmith would like to speak to you." Giving his telephone number, Mr. Goldsmith's secretary requested, "Please return this call at your earliest convenience. Thank you."

When I returned Mr. Goldsmith's call, I was surprised that he was a prospective patient. It is very rare for somebody to ask a secretary to arrange for an appointment with a therapist. Usually therapy is a private and confidential matter and most individuals seeking therapy prefer to make the appointment directly. I reflected on this behavior for awhile and wondered whether he wanted to impress me with his importance. I also thought that he might be uncomfortable about seeking me out by himself; maybe he needed somebody else to take the lead for him.

On the phone Ben Goldsmith started the conversation by telling me he was familiar with some of my writing but quickly went on to say that he himself made a living out of writing. He was an editor of a magazine that dealt with psychological subjects and he pointed out that some of his interests and mine overlapped. Ben Goldsmith certainly did not sound like a prospective patient over the phone. Rather, he came across as an old friend or colleague who wanted to get together to chat over a cup of coffee.

The affable manner I experienced over the telephone was more exaggerated when I met him in the waiting room. A tall, robust, bearded man of about 35, Ben Goldsmith shook my hand with so much vigor that I winced from pain and for the next ten minutes my hand ached. "Hi, hi," he said deeply and loudly. "I'm sorry I'm a little late!" (He was fifteen minutes late for his appointment.)

In the waiting room Ben informed me that he was always trying to meet deadlines in his work; consequently, it was difficult for him to make appointments on time. And, as we walked to my office he told me that he was in the middle of a story about therapists who abuse their patients, insurance companies, and medicaid. (I asked myself, with a little squirming, "Is he afraid I'll abuse him?")

Even after we were seated, I had the impression that Ben was not going to find it easy to discuss the problems that brought him to my office. From his secretary's phone call to his exposé on therapists, Ben was definitely trying to avoid appearing like a person in need. I wondered how much and for how long he would need this defense. I also wondered how suspicious he was of me inasmuch as early in our contact he already had referred to abusive therapists.

After about ten seconds of silence, I told Ben that I was curious to know what prompted him to arrange to see me. I purposely referred to *my* curiosity, feeling that if I exposed some of my own humanness he might reveal some of his. I was only partially correct.

Ben responded to my interest in knowing why he was seeking me out by first smiling and saying, "My profession is one of trying to satisfy people's curiosity. So, I'll try to satisfy yours." He then went on to make an attempt to tell me something about his problems.

"Although women fall in love with me quite easily, I do not easily get turned on to them," Ben began. Continuing, he said, "I think I can call you Herb. You see, Herb, like you I'm an intellectual and I find most women do not match my intellectual rigor. As a result I look down on them and eventually I leave them."

He spent the next fifteen minutes telling me how much he enjoyed having sex with women. Sometimes during the course of one day he could have "three damsels in the sack." "Women love my body and my technique. It's too bad I don't love them," Ben said with a mixture of pride and a little sadness.

In detail, Ben described his many sexual escapades. It was clear that he enjoyed the challenge and the adventure of seducing women. However, it was equally clear that after he had "scored," he lost interest. As I listened to Ben, he appeared more and more to be a Don Juan who viewed women as trophies to be won, rather than as individuals to love and be loved by. I also felt that Ben was frightened of a warm, intimate, human relationship with women. Furthermore, the way he was trying to exhibit his prowess by boasting to me of his sexual achievements was similar to the way he had shown off his professional activities.

Toward the end of our interview, I learned a little about Ben's family life. He was an only child of middle-class parents. His father was an insurance salesman and his mother was an elementary school teacher. When Ben was 13 years old, his father died suddenly of a heart attack. Ben showed little emotion in talking about his father's death. He did say that he remembered his father to be a very busy, intense man who had very little to do with him. Ben turned to an uncle for fatherly affection.

Ben's mother was described as a very affectionate woman who always tried to please Ben. According to him, she didn't have a close relationship with Ben's father and he was surprised that she didn't remarry.

Ben lived at home until after he graduated from college. He majored in journalism at a prominent university in New York City and did very well as a student. Although Ben had lived apart from his mother for well over ten years, he called her daily and saw her weekly.

After I concluded our interview, I told myself that although some of his dynamics seemed quite clear, I thought Ben would be a real challenge to work with. When I noted that I used the word "challenge," it dawned on me that this was the same word Ben used to describe how he felt in seducing a woman. I asked myself, "Do I see Ben as somebody I want to seduce in order to prove my therapeutic prowess?" I thought there was much validity to my hypothesis.

Ben was clearly not eager to form an intimate relationship with me, and despite his superficial warmth, he was quite distant emotionally. I wondered if he would be like his aloof father with me and try to induce me to want him the way he yearned for his father, and the way he arranged for women to want him. As I conjectured further about Ben's dynamics, I had many thoughts about his unresolved oedipal conflict. He was very close to his mother—perhaps too close—and he never had a close relationship with his father. Perhaps he viewed his father's death as an oedipal triumph? And, perhaps when he got emotionally close to women, it felt too incestuous for him? I also wondered if Ben had retreated to a latent homosexual position. He avoided a close intimate relationship with a woman that fused tender and erotic feelings and I thought he may have been still looking for the father he never had. There was also a competitive streak in Ben's demeanor with me. I wondered about this, too.

When I tried to reflect some more about Ben, I had an interesting reaction. I found myself jumping from theorist to theorist, realizing that I was searching for some understanding of Ben that was not coming to me. I thought of Horney's (1950) notion of "basic anxiety" which refers to feeling like a child in a hostile world. I recalled Sullivan's (1953) idea that every child "needs a chum" and if he did not have one in childhood, he would yearn for a chum as an adult, but try to defend against knowing this. And, of course, I also thought of Kohut's (1971, 1977) ideas on narcissism because Ben seemed like Mr. Narcissism himself.

Whenever I find myself moving actively from one theoretical notion to another, I usually recognize some counterresistance at work in myself. (I turned this self-discovery into a paper entitled, "Countertransference and Theoretical Predilections," 1995). What the countertransference issue now seemed to be was that I was feeling a basic anxiety and had to cope with my own feelings of loneliness in the therapeutic situation. I wanted Ben to be my chum, but he was aloof, and this punctured some of my own narcissism. My theoretical preoccupations about Ben, in effect, were thinly disguised projections of my own.

When I could accept with more equanimity some of my own vulnerability and loneliness in dealing with Ben, I began to feel more empathy toward him.

When Ben told me he wanted to see me once a week, he also informed me that he had been in therapy twice before. In both instances, once with a male therapist and once with a female therapist, "there were communication difficulties." Ben described the man as "too arrogant and distant" and the woman as "too eager and enveloping." The descriptions of the therapists sounded like descriptions of his father and mother and I felt quite sure he would transfer some of these characteristics to me. When Ben mentioned that he had left both of his therapists after "just a few months," it also sounded similar to the way he left women after "just a few months."

The Initial Interviews

Ben spent his first ten interviews talking almost exclusively about issues that involved two themes. One was his work; he spent a lot of time telling me about his skills in administration, supervision, and editing. The other theme involved descriptions of his activities with women, with a major emphasis on his sexual escapades. Ben's productions were devoid of fantasies, dreams, and transference reactions. Feeling afraid of revealing his vulnerabilities, he stayed with reality issues (Inderbitzin and Levy 1994).

As I listened to Ben, I realized that mainly he wanted to entertain me and wasn't particularly interested in hearing from me. He seemed quite satisfied with his weekly interviews, always greeting me and taking leave with smiles and warm salutations. It was clear that Ben was relating to me the way he did to women. He was using me to exhibit his potency, but had little interest in his impact on me or in what I may have wanted from him. I began to be concerned about his strong resistance to examining himself, but I was a bit perplexed on how to help him resolve it.

Despite Ben's air of bravado, I knew that below the surface he was a frightened boy. Thus I believed that to confront him with his resistance directly would arouse a lot of anxiety. Yet, I did not want to leave his resistance untouched because that would not help him at all. There-fore, I decided that Ben needed a tactful, soft, but definite confrontation. I said, "Ben, you are very successful on the job and very successful with women. I'm impressed with your success with both. However, I think I might be missing something. Is there something at work or in your relationships with women that I should be addressing?"

Ben smiled and said, "You're a kind fellow! But, I'll tell you what you haven't addressed. It's that I don't get much pleasure from my work or from women." I asked him if this was something we could discuss further. He thought so, but it was clear that though he answered my question affirmatively, there was a lot of reluctance in his voice.

The Transference Resistance

It was during the third month of therapy when Ben told me that if I could help him derive some pleasure from work and love, I would be "a miracle worker." By now it was clear that he had limited respect for psychotherapy and for my ability to help him. I told Ben that although he had been friendly toward me, I believed he had strong doubts about my being useful as a therapist. Ben agreed and spent several sessions expressing his doubts about me and psychotherapy. He suggested that "every man is for himself" and that I really did not care as much about him as a person as I cared about making a living and proving that my theories were correct. He didn't "resent" me too much for my narcissism because that was "the essence of most people."

While Ben was expressing his grave doubts about me and the rest of mankind, I sensed that he was experiencing me as the distant, non-caring father who gave him very little. I also felt that the narcissism he was describing in everyone else was a projection of his own infantile grandiosity. However, I knew he was far from facing psychological truths about himself.

I asked Ben if he had ever had a relationship with anyone that was an exception to the rule. He mentioned his maternal uncle who had taken him to ballgames and played catch with him from time to time. However, this uncle had his own children, and as time went on he'd had little time for Ben.

It was difficult for Ben to acknowledge any disappointment in his uncle who abandoned him the way his father did. And it was next to impossible for Ben to voice any sadness with regard to his father. Yet, as I listened to Ben, I felt sad as I visualized him as a lonely boy who did not receive much love from a father or father figure.

I decided to share some of my countertransference reactions. I told him that when I pictured him growing up, I felt sad. I further told him that when I put myself in his shoes, I felt teary and wanted a strong father to put his arm around me.

I was entirely surprised but a little jarred when Ben became quite angry with me. He told me that I came across as "a weak patsy." I had "no guts," or "real strength" and that I "lacked independence." "The more I think about it, Strean, you might be a fairy," Ben proclaimed.

Realizing that he was projecting his own unacceptable dependency and latent homosexuality onto me, I felt it was important for Ben's therapy that I not be defensive about the characteristics he was perceiving in me. If I could tolerate in myself what Ben couldn't accept in himself, maybe I could help him be less critical of feelings of vulnerability in himself and others. Therefore, when Ben asked belligerently, "Are you gay?" I felt it was important not to affirm or deny it, but to consider it with him. So, I asked, "How would you feel toward me if I were gay?"

In response to my question, Ben again became furious. He told me that he was thinking of leaving treatment now that he "knew" I was gay. When I remained silent, Ben said, "Are you too scared to fight and be a man?" I answered, "Ben, I think that you feel that if a man doesn't fight, he's not a man—he's more like a woman." "Yes," he agreed, and went on to say, "And you are a woman!"

What I was experiencing with Ben at this point in his treatment is not uncommon when working with unattached male patients. Denying their dependency yearnings and wishes to be gratified by a strong father, these men attack the therapist who seems in their minds to be forcing them into a submissive posture. Ben attacked me because he was afraid to love me. He was worried that I might be a woman, because he had to ward off his own wishes to be a woman. My statement about my wanting a father to put an arm around me obviously was overwhelming to him. But, he did not have the guts to admit it.

This stage of therapy with the unattached male can be very tedious for both patient and practitioner. The therapist cannot afford to feel retaliative about the patient's attacks, or too vulnerable about being called a patsy or some other castigating and castrating term.

The Homosexual Transference

Ben continued to castigate me and mock me for a couple of months because he could "not accept" how "terribly unmasculine" I appeared to be. However, when I listened attentively and said little, he began to think more about "the etiology of [my] pathology." As he reflected on my dynamics, Ben was quite sure I had an authoritarian father who gave me "little affection." Therefore, I was always in need of paternal support and couldn't "stand on my own two feet."

While "analyzing" me, Ben tried persistently to engage me in arguments. When he saw that I did not involve myself in the arguments, after voicing some indignation and exasperation, his hardness diminished and he began to show me the little boy in himself who hungered for a father to love him.

It was late in Ben's first year of therapy when he brought in his dream. In the dream Ben was seated on a chair and hugging a little boy on his lap. In associating to his dream, Ben lamented the fact that he was 36 years old and was not a father yet. He believed the dream reflected his wish to be a father and love a son. I told Ben it was my experience in working with men who had received limited fathering that they could vicariously be fathered themselves while nurturing a son. Ben could accept my statement and went on to tell me how much he'd always wanted to be on his father's lap. Sobbing, he said, "I feel so gypped, so lonely, and so vulnerable. If I had a father, I'd be much stronger."

After Ben could acknowledge his wish to be a little boy and be fondled by a father, he began to test out the idea of me being his father. Not only did he begin to fantasize going into private practice with me and becoming a therapist, but he had dreams and fantasies of my adopting him and declaring to the world that he was my son. He was even able to allow himself several direct homosexual dreams and fantasies in which he was sucking my penis and we were having anal intercourse.

While in the midst of a strong homosexual transference, Ben increased his sessions to twice a week. A few months later he began to come three times a week.

Some Reconsiderations about Women

When Ben did not have to hide behind power struggles as a defense (Moses-Hrushovski 1994) and could accept with more equanimity his wishes to be given to, he started to modify his relationships with women. Instead of seeing women exclusively as sexual objects, he began to feel more tenderness toward them.

As he moved toward women, Ben began to talk more about his mother. He realized that he had always had a strong attachment to her and recalled how she really used him as a substitute husband. Into his second year of therapy, Ben recalled a game he had played with her when he was about 10 in which they pretended they were boyfriend and girlfriend. Ben also recalled into his teens helping his mother fasten and unfasten her bra. Furthermore, he told me that throughout his childhood and into the present his mother often walked around the house wearing few clothes or none at all.

As Ben discussed his strong sexual involvement with his mother, he began to see how it played a very large role in his difficulties with women. He could see how he unconsciously arranged to turn women into engulfing mothers and therefore could not feel too close, tender, or intimate with them. In effect, despite his air of bravado with women, he really felt like a little boy who could be easily controlled. Consequently, he ran away from them after defensively proving that he was a conqueror.

The more Ben could talk about his own excitement with his mother, the easier it became for him to feel relaxed with the women he dated. He became less aggressive and exhibitionistic and more loving and object-related. However, there was still something missing. As was true at the beginning of his treatment, Ben was running away from his feelings toward me as he discussed his love affair with his mother.

The Ambivalent Transference

As Ben continued to explore his relationship with his mother, I sensed that he was feeling increasingly uncomfortable. Eventually, we were able to discover that he was apprehensive about my reactions. He was making me the father of his past and was concerned that I would be angry at him for his "success" with his mother. In exploring Ben's transference reactions, it became quite clear that he had had strong competitive fantasies toward his father as he now had toward me. What was particularly important for us to discover was Ben's belief that his aggression could destroy me in the same way he had destroyed his father.

When Ben could face his own death wishes as psychological realities, he began to explore just why he had so much hatred in him. He had not really forgiven his father for being an absent father. He held onto the childish notion that his father had it to give, but merely withheld his love. He also wanted to believe that I could adopt him as my son, but that I was stubborn about it.

"One Woman at Last"

When Ben could accept the reality that his father was a limited man with deep emotional problems rather than just "a cruel father," he became a more soft-spoken, tender human being. He began to relate to me with consistent warmth, admiration, and gratitude.

During the fourth year of treatment, he began to date a

social worker, Millie, on a steady basis. His promiscuous behavior stopped entirely and he constantly reiterated that he was exclusively involved with "one woman at last."

Toward the end of his fourth year of treatment, Ben decided to marry Millie. As he got closer to her he initiated the idea of terminating therapy. Terminating was very painful for Ben. He constantly reminded me and himself that I was "a solid parent" and he would miss having me "on [his] side." I was very touched by Ben's warm appreciation and said I would miss him. When Ben realized that we would both remember each other with much fondness, he was ready to terminate his therapy.

Two years after Ben married Millie, they had a little girl. A year and a half after that they had a son. I hear from Ben annually and he appears to have learned how to love.

8

Counseling
Couples

It is my strong conviction that the individual who has difficulties in sustaining a long-term, one-to-one intimate relationship will profit most from one-to-one long-term psychotherapy. As the patient faces in the transference relationship his chronic complaints, fears, and anxieties, and relives dimensions of his troubled past, the possibility of resolving pertinent personal and interpersonal problems is very much enhanced.

In Chapter 3, I pointed out that some individuals already involved in a relationship and considering marriage may benefit from couples counseling. These may be persons who feel very uncomfortable in individual therapy and resist it strongly. Often they may be part of a symbiotic dyad and cannot separate from their partners. Occasionally, there are certain men and women involved in a stable relationship who can resolve some interpersonal problems in couples counseling. Finally there are some in individual therapy who feel they can gain from couples counseling with a focus on the couple's interaction.

Although many writers and practitioners view couples therapy as the treatment of choice for unattached individuals, I tend to view couples therapy for the unattached individual as either a supplement to or preparation for individual therapy. Very often it is short term.

I would like to present two cases of couples counseling. The first case, Sue and Harry, resolved many of their interpersonal problems as a result of the couples counseling and got married. The second case, Betty and John, after being in couples counseling, decided to break up.

The Case of Sue and Harry

Sue and Harry, both in their middle thirties, had been dating on and off for about four years. During this time, each had been in individual therapy for over two years. Although Sue and Harry had benefited a great deal from individual therapy, neither could feel fully comfortable about becoming committed to each other. By the same token, neither of them wanted to dissolve their relationship.

Sue and Harry were given my name by Sue's former

therapist. When I met them for the first consultation interview, they immediately impressed me as a handsome couple. Sue, a tall, attractive, blonde woman was a director of a public relations firm, and Harry, a tall, bearded man, was chairman of the speech department at a community college. Each of them was well groomed and tastefully dressed.

After we were seated, they smiled at each other and Harry suggested to Sue, "You start first." She replied, "I'd feel better if you started." Harry complied and went on to tell me that he "truly" loved Sue, was very eager to please her, but consistently felt that she was never fully satisfied with him. Harry then looked at Sue and said plaintively, "When I'm talking, I sometimes feel you're not interested. At times when we're making love, I feel you're not there. And you know how often you criticize me. I wish you'd praise me more."

After a silence, Sue began to speak and looking at me commented, "He's right. I am very critical of him. I wish I weren't so critical of Harry, but I am. I wish I could praise him more, but I don't."

As Harry listened to Sue's comments, he seemed to become more and more depressed, but said nothing. At this point, I commented, "Harry, you look depressed. What are you feeling, Sue?" Sue replied, "Oh, I'm depressed too." Then, looking at Harry, she said, "I wish I could love you more. It depresses me that I can't." Harry smiled and said, "If it depresses you not to love me, start loving me and you won't be so depressed." Sue looked annoyed, but remained silent.

I said to Sue, "Harry's last comment seemed to get you angry." Sue acknowledged her anger and said to Harry, "At times I think you're like a little boy asking his mother to love him. I wish you wouldn't depend on me so much. I wish you'd stand on your own two feet more. You seem to want my approval and permission for so many things."

Harry acknowledged that he tended to view Sue as "a mother figure" and went on to talk about his own "cold, self-involved" mother who gave him very little and seemed to appreciate his older brother more. He suggested that he often felt his father preferred his brother, too.

Harry went on to speak at length of his "narcissistic" mother who "never" gave him much acknowledgment but "a great deal of disdain" instead. Tearfully, he commented, "I need you to tell me you value me, but instead you ignore me. You're just like my mother at times."

What Harry was doing at this moment is typical of men and women in unhappy love relationships. They clearly see similarities between the lover or spouse and their own parent, but fail to recognize that they have chosen the mother or father of their pasts in order to fight them. One of the important tasks in marital counseling or couples therapy is helping the patient take responsibility for relating to his or her partner as if he or she were the parent of the past. This, of course, necessitates helping the patient face his or her deep, but usually unconscious, wish to be a child with a parent.

After Harry spoke steadily for about ten minutes about his parents Sue chimed in, "And you'd like me to make up for your past. Well, I'm not your mother or father and that's hard for you to realize, Harry." She then turned to me and said that her parents were separated when she was 10 years old. She often had to rely on her own resources and couldn't depend on anybody too much. "Neither of my parents had much to offer," Sue said angrily.

By the middle of the session I began to develop several hypotheses and impressions of Sue and Harry. Their relationship appeared in many ways like that of mother and son. Harry was intimidated by Sue and kept trying to please her. Never feeling that he received her approbation, he kept on trying. Sue, on the other hand, seemed to be frightened of a close relationship with Harry and needed to knock him down in order to maintain distance. However, I thought that she must have enjoyed Harry's persistence; otherwise, she would not have continued the relationship.

The more I thought about it, Sue and Harry were trapped in a collusion. Harry was constantly trying to please his woman who did not want to be pleased. In effect, Harry did not feel like an autonomous and potent man, and Sue constantly verified this for him. Sue needed to believe a man was weak and impotent and that she was stronger, and Harry constantly verified this for her.

Toward the end of the interview, I shared my overall impression of their interaction. I told Sue and Harry that they struck me as bright and vigorous individuals and that each had many strengths. I also could detect warm feelings between them. But, I pointed out the struggle I thought they were in. Harry was trying desperately to please Sue who found it hard to be pleased and Sue seemed to find it uncomfortable to feel close to Harry. They nodded approvingly at my remarks and agreed to meet with me weekly.

For the next three sessions, Harry and Sue tended to act out the conflict we identified. Harry brought in examples of trying to please Sue, which only succeeded in antagonizing her. When Harry saw that Sue was irritated, he would try harder to please her and she tried harder to push him away.

During their sixth session, I told Sue and Harry that they must be getting some kind of protection from the collusion they formed. I suggested that he must get something from being rejected so constantly, and she must get something from being displeased constantly.

Sue did not like my comment and said, "I don't get anything out of being displeased. That's ridiculous. That's a lot of therapeutic mumbo jumbo." Harry proceeded to tell Sue and me that we really agreed and there was just "a mild difficulty in communication." Sue told Harry his comments were "ridiculous," just as mine were.

I was able to show Sue and Harry that what was happening in our session occurred in their daily interactions. Sue was pushing Harry and me away, and Harry was trying to please both of us. Sue smiled and said, "I hate to agree with you, Herb, but you're right." She then gave several examples of wanting to argue with men to show she was "somebody of worth" and that this was a lifelong problem of hers. Harry then confessed that if he could really believe he was somebody of worth, he would not need so much reaffirmation from Sue.

When Sue and Harry became more aware of the neurotic component of their relationship, they became less tense with each other. They both recalled discussing the issues we were working on in their individual therapy. Harry talked about his fear of his aggression, particularly toward women, and about his dread that Sue would leave him if he asserted himself. Sue talked about her rage at her father and toward other men because she never felt fully appreciated as a girl or a woman.

When Sue and Harry could both acknowledge their individual conflicts and how they impacted on each other, they began to talk about their sexual difficulties with each other. Sue, at first, stated with impatience and anger, "If you didn't come so fast, I'd have some fun." To this Harry blushed deeply and then asked for some forgiveness and tolerance from Sue. When she responded to his discomfort with disdain, he was able to assert himself with a degree of "potency." He commented, "If you want to fight and insult me, it won't help either of us in bed." Sensing Harry's increased strength, Sue was able to show some respect and said, "I think we're acting out our sex life in front of Herb. Instead of loving nicely, we're tense and angry."

What Sue perceived in the session was a helpful hint to all therapists who do couples counseling. If the couple is having difficulty in their sex life, help them observe how they communicate in the sessions. As both individuals face their hurts, resentments, and other issues directly and honestly with each other, it is psychologically equivalent to getting undressed in front of each other and empathizing with each other. This experience of being psychologically undressed is often a helpful "dress rehearsal" for good sex.

As Harry became less of a suffering boy trying to please Sue, he could relax more sexually. Concomitantly, Sue acknowledged that as she could better face her war with men, she could relax more with Harry "in and out of bed."

After five months of couples counseling, Sue and Harry decided to live together. Both thought they could work on their individual issues in their individual therapy. After they reestablished their individual therapies, they stopped couples counseling, and after each of them had been in individual therapy for close to a year, they married. Reports on their marital relationship continued to be positive.

The Case of Betty and John

Betty and John had been dating for about three years. During this time, they lived separately but when they came to see me, they were considering living together. They were referred to me by a friend who had been in couples counseling with me. At the time of referral, both were in individual therapy. John was a conductor for a symphony orchestra and Betty was a flutist in the orchestra.

When I met John and Betty in the waiting room, they

were both dressed in casual clothes and both had serious expressions on their faces. John was a middling tall man in his forties. Betty was 30, a little shorter than John, and took the lead in introducing themselves.

In my office, Betty again took the lead in beginning the session. She told me that during the time she and John had been dating they had had many arguments and separations. They were afraid that if they did make the move to live together, they would both regret it.

When I saw that John did not respond to Betty's remarks and that Betty had nothing further to say at the moment, I thought I would intervene. "Let's see if we can understand better how you feel right now about living together." To my comment, John shook his head as if disapproving of the idea and Betty appeared sad and somewhat tense. I then shared my impressions. "John, you're shaking your head at the idea of living together, and Betty, you look sad and a bit concerned."

John acknowledged that he was "a bit uptight" about living with Betty. He had already been in one marriage for three years "that didn't work out" and he was worried "it would happen again." To this, Betty remarked that she wasn't the same kind of person that John's first wife was and that she could make life better for him.

"You may be right," said John to Betty, "but I still worry that we'll have our arguments and make each other miserable."

John and Betty spent most of the remainder of the session arguing. John accused Betty of wanting too much from him, his "constant presence," his "availability to always converse," and his "constant reassurance." Betty accused John of wanting little to do with her "except for sex" and that was why she "needed the reassurance" she frequently requested. John then told Betty that if she complained less, he could give her more, to which Betty replied, "If you gave me more, I'd bother you less!"

I learned from John and Betty that they came from homes where the parents divorced when both were around 8 or 9 years old and each had one older brother. Each recalled tense home atmospheres with their parents arguing frequently, threatening divorce constantly, and separating from each other occasionally.

Though I was not completely certain, even after just one interview I did not feel too optimistic about Betty and John's future together. Despite the fact that their interpersonal conflicts were not unusual, what was striking was their mutual rigidity. Neither seemed capable of taking responsibility for what he or she was doing to alienate the other. Both were very critical of each other and seemed devoid of empathy. I particularly wondered about the weakness of their object relations—a necessary ego function to resolve interpersonal conflicts.

For the next five or six sessions, John and Betty argued bitterly. Not only did they echo the same sentiments voiced in their initial consultation, but each accused the other of trying to defeat their relationship. To compound difficulties, they both quoted their individual therapists to add fuel to their arguments.

Whenever I tried to intervene in the sessions, I was either ignored or interrupted. During the twelfth session I called this to their attention and said, "It's very difficult for you to listen to each other, and you know I don't think it's easy for either of you to listen to me." In response to my comment, John first accused Betty of not listening and then Betty did the same thing to him. When I tried to show them that they were berating rather than trying to understand each other, they argued some more.

What I saw happening with Betty and John was something I have seen a great deal in individual therapy—the "negative therapeutic reaction" (Freud 1923). When Freud coined this term, he was talking about the patient who, despite absorbing many interpretations, never made any progress. Freud ascribed this lack of therapeutic movement to a punitive superego—the patient felt too guilty to allow any forward movement in the therapy. As other clinicians dealt with the negative therapeutic reaction (for example, Fine 1982, Strean 1990), they acknowledged the guilt but suggested that the patient wants to spite and defeat the therapist's attempts to help him or her.

At their seventeenth session, I told John and Betty that each of them seemed to have a stake in fighting with each other, defeating each other, and defeating me, as well. Characteristically, Betty claimed this was true of John, and John was sure this was true of Betty.

Whatever I said or they said to each other they seemed to use in the service of a fight. In contrast to many other couples who fight during the sessions but behave much more constructively outside, Betty and John derided each other daily in and out of therapy.

I was not successful trying to understand John and

Betty's power struggles. Even when I shared some of my countertransference reactions (which I thought might prove helpful), they were able to defeat me. In their twenty-eighth session I told Betty and John that I felt their wish to defeat each other and me was stronger than my wish to help them. To this John replied, "Nothing works with us," and Betty promptly disagreed and involved him in another sadomasochistic orgy. On my saying to them, "I think if I gave you the correct time, you'd end up arguing about it. John laughed and Betty characteristically said, "There's nothing funny about this."

Around their thirtieth session, John told Betty and me that his therapist had advised him to break up with Betty because it was making both of them miserable. Although Betty had some reservations about this advice, she was so bitter that she just walked out of the session and I never heard from her again.

John did call me a couple of times to tell me he had a new girlfriend and that he was getting along with her much better than he had with Betty.

The case of John and Betty was one of my most outstanding failures, in that no progress of any kind occurred. I realize that a therapist cannot help everybody. We all have our limitations and that is why, like our patients, we are all "more human than otherwise."

9

Summary and Conclusions

This book was written for the mental health professional. By focusing on the unique dynamics and treatment of the unattached patient, I hope to help the practitioner gain more expertise and comfort in working with his or her modal patient—the single, divorced, or widowed man or woman.

When I embarked on this project, I took the unequivocal position that the unattached person, despite his or her rationalizations, has a strong yearning to love and be loved. He or she would very much like to become attached, but fears, anxieties, inhibitions, character defenses, symptoms, and some weak ego functions prevent him or her from consummating a relationship.

Although many of the psychodynamics and treatment procedures that relate to unattached patients overlap with the diagnosis and therapy of other patients, including those who are attached and married, I have tried in this book to focus on what is particularly crucial in the assessment and treatment of the single, divorced, or widowed patient.

My review of the existing but sparse clinical research on the unattached clearly demonstrated that unattached individuals are more lonely than the rest of the population. They die earlier, show more neurotic symptoms, particularly bodily symptoms such as heart disease, are more suicidal, and they outnumber other categories of patients in outpatient mental health clinics, family agencies, and mental hospitals.

Before we embarked on the clinical phase of this project, it was important to examine certain historical and cultural variables pertinent to our study. Despite the fact that marriage has always tended to be idealized, ever since Adam and Eve and through most of the twentieth century, there has never been a golden age of marriage. The idea of fusing tender and erotic feelings and expressing these feelings in a sustained, monogamous relationship has been a task most men and women have not been able to master very well. One of the main reasons for this is that most individuals tend to make their partners parental figures. Consequently, old parent–child conflicts reappear in the marital relationship, and sexual contact begins to be experienced as forbidden incest.

With the aforementioned historical and cultural variables in mind, it is not too difficult to understand why many individuals resist marriage, and why more people in our society postpone or reject marriage entirely. The numbers of the unattached in our society keep soaring. Although it is less socially taboo to be unattached, the many unattached men and women who frequent psychotherapists' offices do not enjoy being single, divorced, or widowed. The majority of mental health professionals concur that the unattached want a partner.

Despite the fact that all unattached individuals are conditioned by contemporary folkways and mores, in order to individualize the unattached patient in psychotherapy, I concluded that it was imperative to get a comprehensive picture of his or her psychosexual development. In the vignettes of Chapter 2, the psychosexual development of unattached patients showed many impairments. Most frequently, these patients did not witness their parents enjoying each other. Rather, the parents had many interpersonal difficulties of their own. They were poor role models for their developing children.

The case histories in Chapters 2 through 8 specified the kinds of difficulties that beset unattached patients. Some of them did not receive sufficient tender love and care during the oral period and therefore could not trust a partner. Rather, they became paranoid with their partners and often projected their oral hunger, narcissism, grandiosity, and infantile omnipotence onto their partners. Not infrequently, they emerged as demanding babies and alienated their partners.

Many of the unattached patients were involved in severe

power struggles that prevented them from loving and being loved by a partner. To love or to be loved by a partner
made them feel as if they were "doing their duty" for a
parent. This activated a great deal of resentment and was
acted out in sexual relations, decision making, and elsewhere. It certainly squelched intimacy and spontaneity.

Virtually all unattached patients had unresolved gender
problems, feeling anxiety as men or women and not able
to fully accept themselves with their biological givens. In
addition many patients under examination had severe
oedipal difficulties. They tended to view their partners as
parental figures and felt like children next to them. This
resulted in many sexual and emotional difficulties.

In Chapter 3 I discussed some of the important therapeutic principles involved. Although many of these principles are pertinent to the treatment of other patients, they
are crucial in the treatment of the single, divorced, or
widowed patient.

A very important concept in the treatment of the
unattached patient is that every chronic complaint of the
partner is an unconscious wish. The man who complains
that his partner is "a cold bitch" unconsciously desires
such a partner. If he were involved with a warm woman,
he would become anxious. Similarly, the woman who
complains that her boyfriend is a weak boy unconsciously
wants a weak boy. A potent man would scare her.

The best way to help unattached patients lessen their
complaints, discover their unconscious wishes, and recognize their maladaptive defenses is to study their transference reactions to the therapist. If the therapist maintains a

neutral but empathetic position, invariably the patient will experience the therapist the same way he or she experiences the partner. Helping the patient become aware of transference reactions enables him to gain some conviction that he relates in a maladaptive way in every intimate relationship. With this conviction, most patients reduce their hatred and try to love.

Just as the study of transference reactions to the therapist helped my patients gain more understanding and mastery of the way they related to their partners, a study of their resistances had a similar effect. The resistances my patients showed in the treatment situation, for example, arguing with the therapist, ingratiation, and denying emotions, tended to be used in a similar manner in their intimate relationships.

In working with the unattached a constant study by the therapist of his or her own countertransference responses is imperative. Because the patient's main difficulty is usually in interpersonal relationships, the therapist must know how much therapeutic activity is governed by what the patient truly needs and how much is expressed to help the therapist lower anxiety and/or gratify subjective wishes.

We also learned that when therapists constantly study the feelings and thoughts their patients induce in them, they learn what the patient is unconsciously seeking, for example, to seduce, to battle, to compete. Sometimes these reactions can be shared with the patient.

Throughout this book I was wedded to the notion that one-to-one long-term treatment is the therapy of choice for the unattached patient. Nonetheless, for those patients who strongly resist individual treatment, couples counseling can be helpful. Those patients who are very symbiotic and cannot separate may need couples counseling as a preparation for or supplement to individual therapy. Other patients, such as those in individual treatment, may profit from couples counseling when they focus exclusively on their interaction with their partners. However, it is important for the therapist and patient to consider fully the request to go into couples counseling because it may indicate that the patient is expressing some form of resistance to his or her individual therapy.

Psychotherapy for the unattached men and women, with a focus on their psychosexual development, and with adherence to dynamic concepts in the therapy such as transference, countertransference, resistance, and counterresistance can help many lonely, angry individuals become able to enjoy a warm, intimate, and pleasureful relationship with a loving partner.

References

Abend, S. (1982). Serious illness in the analyst: countertransference considerations. *Journal of the American Psychoanalytic Association* 30:365–379.

———— (1989). Countertransference and psychoanalytic technique. *Psychoanalytic Quarterly* 58: 374–393.

Ables, B. (1977). *Therapy for Couples*. San Francisco: Jossey-Bass.

Ackerman, N. (1958). *The Psychodynamics of Family Life*. New York: Basic Books.

Barker, R. (1984). *Treating Couples in Crisis*. New York: Free Press.

Bergler, E. (1963). Marriage and divorce. In *A Handbook of Psychoanalysis*, ed. H. Herma and G. Kurth, pp. 186–206. Cleveland, OH: World.

Bloch, M. (1961). *Feudal Society*. Chicago: University of Chicago Press.

Blos, P. (1967). The second individuation process of adolescence. In *Psychoanalytic Study of the Child*, 22:162–186. New York: International Universities Press.

Bowlby, J. (1973). *Separation*. New York: Basic Books.

Brenner, C. (1985). Countertransference as compromise formation. *Psychoanalytic Quarterly* 54:155–163.

DeBurger, J. (1978). *Marriage Today*. Cambridge, MA: Schenkman.

DeMause, L. (1981). *Foundations of Psychohistory*. New York: Creative Roots.

Demos, J. (1976). Myths and realities in the history of American family life. In *Contemporary Marriage: Structure, Dynamics and Therapy*, ed. H. Grunebaum and J. Christ, pp. 9–32. Boston: Little, Brown.

Durbin, K. (1977). On sexual jealousy. In *Jealousy*, ed. G. Clanton and L. Smith, pp. 36–46. Englewood Cliffs, NJ: Prentice Hall.

Eisenstein, V. (1956). *Neurotic Interaction in Marriage*. New York: Basic Books.

Ellis, H. (1907). *Studies in the Psychology of Sex*. New York: Random House.

Erikson, E. (1950). *Childhood and Society*. New York: W. W. Norton.

Esman, A. (1979). Adolescence and the new sexuality. In *On Sexuality*, ed. T. Karasu and C. Socarides, pp. 19–28. New York: International Universities Press.

Fine, R. (1968). Interpretation: the patient's response. In *Uses of Interpretation in Treatment: Technique and Art*, ed. E. Hammer, pp. 110–120. New York: Grune and Stratton.

—— (1975). *Psychoanalytic Psychology*. New York: Jason Aronson.

—— (1981). *The Psychoanalytic Vision*. New York: Free Press.

—— (1982). *The Healing of the Mind*. 2nd edition. New York: Free Press.

_____ (1985). *The Meaning of Love in Human Experience.* New York: John Wiley and Sons.

_____ (1988). *Troubled Men.* San Francisco. Jossey-Bass.

_____ (1992). *Troubled Women.* San Francisco: Jossey-Bass.

Fisher, H. (1993). *Anatomy of Love: The Mysteries of Mating and Why We Stray.* New York: Fawcett Columbine.

Fogel, G., Lane, F., and Liebert, R. (1986). *The Psychology of Men.* New York: Basic Books.

Freud, A. (1958). Adolescence. In *Psychoanalytic Study of the Child*, 13:255–278. New York: International Universities Press.

_____ (1965). *Normality and Pathology in Childhood: Assessment of Development.* New York: International Universities Press.

Freud, S. (1896). Further remarks on the neuro-psychoses of defense. *Standard Edition* 3:159–185.

_____ (1905). Three essays on the theory of sexuality. *Standard Edition* 7:125–243.

_____ (1914). On narcissism. *Standard Edition* 14:67–102.

_____ (1923). The ego and the id. *Standard Edition* 19:1–66.

_____ (1926). Inhibitions, symptoms, and anxiety. *Standard Edition* 20:77–174.

_____ (1939). An outline of psychoanalysis. *Standard Edition* 23:141–204.

Friedman, R. (1988). *Male Homosexuality: A Contemporary Psychoanalytic Perspective.* New Haven: Yale University Press.

Garrett, A. (1951). *Interviewing: Its Principles and Methods.* New York: Family Service Association of America.

Gelles, R. (1972). *The Violent Home.* Beverly Hills, CA: Sage.

Greenson, R. (1967). *The Technique and Practice of Psychoanalysis.* New York: International Universities Press.

Grunebaum, H., and Christ, J., eds. (1976). *Contemporary Marriage: Structure, Dynamics, and Therapy.* Boston: Little, Brown.

Grunebaum, H., Christ, J., and Neiberg, N. (1969) Diagnosis

and treatment planning for couples. *International Journal of Group Psychotherapy* 19:185–202.

Hall, C., and Lindzey, G. (1957). *Theories of Personality*. New York: John Wiley and Sons.

Hamilton, G. (1951). *Theory and Practice of Social Casework*. New York: Columbia University Press.

Hay, M. (1975). *Thy Brother's Blood*. New York: Hart.

Hendin, H. (1975). *The Age of Sensation*. New York: W. W. Norton.

Hite, S. (1983). *The Hite Report on Female Sexuality*. New York: Knopf.

Horney, K. (1950). *Neurosis and Human Growth*. New York: W. W. Norton.

Howard, J. (1978). *Families*. New York: Simon and Schuster.

Hunt, M. (1959). *The Natural History of Love*. New York: Knopf.

Inderbitzin, L., and Levy, S. (1994). On grist for the mill: reality as defense. *Journal of the American Psychoanalytic Association* 42: 763–788.

Isay, R. (1989). *Being Homosexual: Gay Men and Their Development*. New York: Farrar, Straus, and Giroux.

Kadushin, A. (1972). *The Social Work Interview*. New York: Columbia University Press.

Kohut, H. (1970). *The Analysis of the Self*. New York: International University Press.

——— (1977). *The Restoration of the Self*. New York: International Universities Press.

Kaplan, H. (1983). *The Evaluation of Sexual Disorders*. New York: Brunner/Mazel.

Langley, R., and Levy, R. (1977). *Wife Beating: The Silent Crisis*. New York: Dutton.

Langs, R. (1981). *Resistances and Interventions*. New York: Jason Aronson.

Lasch, C. (1978). *The Culture of Narcissism*. New York: W. W. Norton.

Lynch, J. (1977). *The Broken Heart*. New York: Basic Books.

Mahler, M. (1968). *On Human Symbiosis and the Vicissitudes of Individuation*. New York: International Universities Press.

Malinowski, M. (1922). *Argonauts of the Western Pacific*. New York: Dutton.

Martin, P. (1976). *A Marital Therapy Manual*. New York: Brunner/Mazel.

Mead, M. (1935). *Sex and Temperament in Three Primitive Societies*. New York: New American Library.

Meissner, W. (1978). The conceptualization of marriage and family dynamics from a psychoanalytic perspective. In *Marriage and Marital Therapy*, ed. T. Paolino and B. McCrady, pp. 25–88. New York: Brunner/Mazel.

Montagu, A. (1956). Marriage—a cultural perspective. In *Neurotic Interaction in Marriage*, ed. V. Eisenstein, pp. 3–9. New York: Basic Books.

Moore, B., and Fine, B. (1990). *Psychoanalytic Terms*. New Haven: Yale University Press.

Moses-Hrushovski, R. (1994). *Development: Hiding Behind Power Struggles as a Character Defense*. Northvale, NJ: Jason Aronson.

Perlman, H. (1957). *Social Casework: A Problem Solving Process*. Chicago: University of Chicago Press.

Reik, T. (1941). *Masochism in Modern Man*. New York: Grove.

Rogers, C. (1951). *Client-Centered Therapy*. Boston: Houghton Mifflin.

Roheim, G. (1952). *The Gates of the Dream*. New York: International Universities Press.

Rohner, R. P. (1975). *They Love Me, Love Me Not*. New Haven: HRAF.

Sable, P. (1994). Anxious attachment in adulthood: therapeutic implications. *Journal of Analytic Social Work* 2(1):5–24.

Seagraves, R. (1982). *Marital Therapy: A Combined Psychodynamic-Behavioral Approach*. New York: Plenum.

Searles, H. (1979). *Countertransference and Related Subjects*. New York: International Universities Press.

Serban, G. (1981). Interview. In *Frontiers of Psychiatry*, vol. 11, no. 9, October 15, 1981, p. 1.

Shachter, B., and Seinfeld, J. (1994). Personal violence and the culture of violence. *Social Work* 39(4):347–350.

Shorter, E. (1975). *The Making of the Modern Family*. New York: Basic Books.

Siporin, M. (1975). *Introduction to Social Work Practice*. New York: Macmillan.

Slakter, E. (1987). *Countertransference*. Northvale, NJ: Jason Aronson.

Smith, J., and Smith, L. (1974). *Beyond Monogamy*. Baltimore: Johns Hopkins University Press.

Socarides, C. (1978). *Homosexuality*. New York: Jason Aronson.

Spitz, R. (1965). *The First Year of Life*. New York: International Universities Press.

Stein, H., and Cloward, R. (1958). *Social Perspectives on Behavior*. Glencoe, IL: Free Press.

Stone, L. (1979). *The Family, Sex, and Marriage in England 1500–1800*. New York: Harper Colophon Books.

Strean, H. (1978). *Clinical Social Work*. New York: Free Press.

——— (1984a). Psychosexual disorders. In *Adult Psychopathology*, ed. F. Turner, pp. 316–345. New York: Free Press.

——— (1984b). Homosexuality: A life-style, a civil rights issue, or a psychosocial problem? *Current Issues in Psychoanalytic Practice* 1(3):35–48.

——— (1985). *Resolving Marital Conflicts*. New York: John Wiley and Sons.

——— (1990). *Resolving Resistances in Psychotherapy*. New York: Brunner/Mazel.

——— (1991). *Behind the Couch: Revelations of a Psychoanalyst*. New York: Continuum.

_____ (1993a). *Resolving Counterresistances in Psychotherapy*. New York: Brunner/Mazel.

_____ (1993b). *Therapists Who Have Sex with Their Patients*. New York: Brunner/Mazel.

_____ (1994). *Essentials of Psychoanalysis*. New York: Brunner/ Mazel.

_____ (1995). Countertransference and theoretical predilections. *Canadian Journal of Psychoanalysis* (in press).

Sullivan, H. S. (1953). *The Interpersonal Theory of Psychiatry*. New York: W. W. Norton.

_____ (1972). *Personal Psychopathology*. New York: W. W. Norton.

Winnicott, D. (1971). *Therapeutic Consultations in Child Psychiatry*. New York: Basic Books.

Index

About the Author

Dr. Herbert Strean is Director of the New York Center for Psychoanalytic Training and Distinguished Professor Emeritus, Rutgers University. He is the author of thirty books and over one hundred professional papers. Some of his popular books are *Behind the Couch, Resolving Resistances in Psychotherapy, Resolving Counterresistances in Psychotherapy, Our Wish to Kill, Resolving Marital Conflict, The Use of Humor in Psychotherapy,* and *Psychotherapy of the Orthodox Jew.*

In his forty years of professional practice, Dr. Strean has trained over 4,000 therapists. He has been on the editorial board of *Psychoanalytic Review, Clinical Social Work,* and *Analytic Social Work,* and is currently Editor-in-Chief of *Current Issues in Psychoanalytic Practice.* Dr. Strean maintains a private practice in New York City.